MAN OF FAITH

Judith Carol Glavosek - Priest

MAN OF FAITH

First Publication:
Published in the United States of America
Published by
ATC Publishing, LLC
P.O. Box 127
Senoia, Georgia 30276

ISBN: 978-1736222225

DEDICATION

Joseph Harry Glavosek
1946 - 1991

*This Book and Pictures are dedicated to our Children,
Grandchildren and to our Later Generations in Hope
They will know who he was and what kind of man he
was throughout his lifetime.*

Table of Contents

INTRODUCTION

This book started out as a gift for my Grandchildren to get to know their Birth Grandfather and the man he was - Overcomer, Achiever and Believer who Never said "I Can't!" Instead, he would say "watch me!"

With the exception of our first Granddaughter Kira, none of the others would ever know him.

Kira was 5 years old at the time so he got to know her, his Granddaughter, his 'Little Princess…''Little Miss Can Do Nothing Wrong' in her Papa's eyes. To this day she has precious memories of her 'Papa'.

Over coffee one Sunday morning a few years back, I contemplated the possibility of creating a book that I could give each of our Grandchildren. It would be a book of true stories, the good and the bad, with pictures of his and 'Our' Life and Times together.

I went about the morning getting ready for Church, having breakfast and thought nothing more about it.

However, while at Church I believe God gave me a message. I cannot remember what the Sermon was about but it felt like the Pastor was speaking directly to me.

I heard the 'message' that I should write and publish the book and name it 'Man of Faith.'

Wow that really hit me!

The 'Message' gave me a very strong feeling that God was talking to me, I could not ignore it. If God tells you to do something, I guess you better take notice and do it!

It's taken me quite a few years and a lot of tears to complete, but here it is, written from my Heart to Yours.

The origin of the Title has an amazing story as well.

Years ago, while Harry was in his last few weeks of Life, Jim Stagg, a Deacon from Holy Trinity Church in Peachtree City, Georgia, visited him regularly.

During that time, Jim and Harry formed a 'Brother in Christ Friendship'.

About a week after Harry passed, Jim gave me a Poem he had written about Harry which really touched me.

How many people do we know would hand you a Poem they'd written about your Loved one?

The name of the Poem is

'Man of Faith'

A Brief Lineage and History of

Joseph Harry Glavosek

Joseph Harry Glavosek was Born July 2, 1945 in Cleveland, Ohio, the son of Paul Glavosek and Marie Owens-Glavosek.

The Glavosek name originated in Croatia where there remain some distant Relatives.

One of them sent as a gift this beautiful Hand-Woven Tapestry from their Country:

Harry had three brothers: Randy Glavosek, Mike Glavosek, and Tom Glavosek, one sister Ruth Glavosek - Albright

He married Judith Carol Albright 1965 in Strongsville, Ohio. They were happily married for 26 years.

Harry and 'Judy' had three children –

- •Joseph Harry Glavosek Jr.
- •Richard Michael Glavosek
- •Paula Michelle Glavosek

Joseph, Paula and Richard

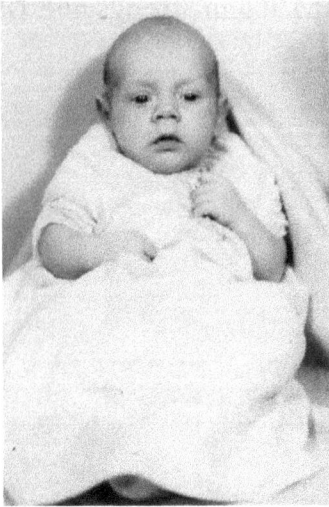

CHAPTER 1

EARLY YEARS

Harry was a hard-working young man who had to find his way through the 'school of hard knocks'.

He did of course make mistakes along the way as we all do.

He pretty much raised himself as sadly his family was very dysfunctional and many times had displaced family members.

His father, Paul was an alcoholic.

Many times, their Mom, Marie had to support all five children by herself working odd jobs and long hours.

Very often she and the children lived with their Grandmother, Marie's Mom, Grandma Owens. She was a very strict, stern and Faithful Catholic.

Harry became very close to his Grandmother and she him. I believe she is the one to instill in him his love for God and his strong faith.

Also, many times, Harry would stay with his Aunt Millie and Uncle Ervin. Uncle Ervin was Harry's mom's brother.

Millie adored Harry and would have loved to adopt him as their own and expressed that often.

Paul and Marie divorced early on due to Paul's drinking. Poor Harry even though he was not the oldest child, did his best to see that his brothers and sister were taken care of. He took on the roll as their caregiver even at this early age. He carried that on, in one way or another, all through his life.

1

If any family member was ever in need of anything, they always looked to Harry for the rescue. He happily obliged if at all in his power to do so.

Early on while he was in middle school, that sometimes meant that he had to steal food or whatever necessity they needed. As they had very little money, he had to file down pennies to drop in the laundromat coin box to do their laundry.

After a time that didn't go to well for Harry as he was caught 'red handed' one day at the Laundromat while doing his own laundry.

Harry was put on probation and later was sent to a Boy's Home for a year and a half. It was extremely hard for him to be away from his family at such a young age.

He vowed that when he got out, he would never return there, which he never did. Even though his own probation officer said to him, "You'll be back, your kind always comes back."

Harry told him that he was wrong! He would not be back!

When he was released from the Boys Industrial School, he knew he needed to find a real job now to help support his family. That meant he couldn't go back to regular school.

He had only been through the 8th grade, started the 9th several times. (You would never know his formal education level as he was very intelligent and had excellent common sense and was always on the leading edge of new technologies.)

He studied and learned the Auto Body Repair and Painting Trade, a trade that would make him a very good living throughout his adult life.

He started out at a small body shop as a Porter and soon worked his way up the ranks. He was a quick learner and a

Perfectionist and very determined to make a difference in his life.

He started living on his own in his late teens and shared his first apartment in Downtown Cleveland, Ohio with his buddy, Roger Carson.

Their apartment was close to work at a shop called Suburban Auto Body.

He worked hard during the week and attended Church most Sunday mornings.

During that time, he helped his Mom, Dad, Brothers and Sister as best he could financially and any way he could.

Don't get me wrong, he was a young man and did his share of partying, he was not a saint for sure. After all he was still a Teenager and learning his way in life.

One thing he knew for sure, he did not want to live a life of poverty ever again, and to achieve that, he knew it was up to him to make a good life for himself.

He did that only through hard work and determination.

Many years later after we were married, he did by chance run into that Probation Officer.

Harry had worked his way up to Manager at Heintzelman Chevrolet at the time, when low and behold, in walked the Guy who said "He would never amount to anything".

Thank you, God, for showing his Probation Officer he was wrong about this hard working and ambitious young man.

It was during those early years, we met each other and fell in Love. That was in 1962. He was 17 and I was 16. We'd met at a little place in Willoughby, Ohio called Teen Town, a Dance Club where Teenagers could hang out and dance the night away with live local bands. A few nights there appeared soon to be famous ones such as the Everly Brothers.

It was during one of those evenings Harry asked me to dance. I didn't even know his name or he mine, but of course I accepted as he was really a good-looking guy, leather coat and all. I found out later that he'd borrowed his coat from a buddy.

We danced and talked the rest of the night and learned each other's names. He asked for my phone number and shortly thereafter we began dating. The song that was being played when we danced our very first dance was "Stardust". That song forever more has been our song.

On one of our first dates.

Easter Morning on our way to Church.

We were still dating when this picture was taken.

We'd been dating for three years when Harry asked me to marry him.

Of course, I accepted and we were married in 1965.

Our Wedding was small but beautiful with close Family and a few friends.

It was a sweet and Special Day that I will Always Treasure Near and Dear to my Heart, March 6, 1965. Our beginning of married life together. So glad I didn't miss that dance!

TORNADO IN STRONGSVILLE, OHIO

One of the first big events that happened the first year we were married was a devastating Tornado.

We were temporarily staying at my Mom and Dads' home in Strongsville, Ohio while waiting for a 2-bedroom duplex we'd leased. It would be a few weeks before it became available.

My Sister, Marlene was still living at home at the time, but my Brother Ken, in March, had left for Army Boot Camp at Fort Knox, Kentucky. We had taken over his empty bedroom for a bit.

On Palm Sunday, April 11, 1965 in the afternoon, we visited with my Brother and Sister-in-law, Allen & Phyllis Albright. It was a beautiful warm and sunny day, couldn't have been nicer!

We arrived back home, had dinner with the family, watched a little TV and turned in. Just a quiet evening, or so we thought.

Then shortly after 11pm we heard our 2 dogs (Peanut and Spider) outside barking their heads off. Dad went outside to see what was the matter with them, he hurriedly ran back into the house and yelled for everyone to get down and away from the windows. By this time, it had been storming for a bit, a real bad storm.

Suddenly, it sounded like a train coming toward us, then, suddenly, it stopped, in an instant!

Moments before, as one lightning bolt struck, I could see other homes outside our window. The next lightning strike, there were no homes. It was deadly quiet.

This all happened in just minutes. As quickly as it came it went away. Just light rain was left. We had no power and the phone lines were down.

Each one of us had our own little story: As I was looking out the bedroom window, Harry dove to the floor and yelled for me to get under the bed with him, Dad hung onto the wall between the garage and kitchen, Mom walked around not knowing what to do still holding her bowl of ice cream and Marlene slept through most of it.

It was all over so quickly.

It was about 11:20pm when this Category F4 Tornado struck and quickly wiped out most of Strongsville, especially the Westwood Estates area.

Our home was on Westwood Drive, however miraculously the only damage we had was to Dad and Harrys cars and to the garage door. Both car antennas were clipped off as huge piece of plywood flew into and through the garage door.

Most people were not that lucky.

Sadly, one tragedy was a baby picked up in her crib and landing in a tree, killing the baby. That was the one fatality in Strongsville, Ohio! However, many homes and businesses were totally destroyed.

Outside looked like a war zone. Harry and Dad tried to go outside to assess the damage but that turned out to be too dangerous. Powerlines were down everywhere. What they could see is there were no standing homes around us and everything was dead silent. Maybe the people were all in shock.

Out back, they saw that both dog houses were missing. Looking closer, both our dogs, Peanut and Spider were gone as well!

That Tornado ranked as one of the deadliest in Ohio history as it ran through several Counties, leaving many homeless and killing over 200 people.

President Johnson, declared this a Major Disaster and brought in the National Guard.

Sometime the next day the Red Cross came to our door making sure we were all ok. It seemed that several Family members had been trying to call, couldn't reach us and of course needed to know if we were ok.

Later that afternoon, my brother Al and sister-in-law Phyllis made their way to us. They had driven as far as they could and continued the rest of the way on foot to our home.

Al took some home movies of the area however it seems no one else did. Everyone was in shock and caught up in recovery from this disastrous event.

Thank you, God, for watching over our family!

MOM AND DAD, FRANK AND MARGARET STEEBER

It just seemed appropriate that I show my Parents following the Tornado story. The pictures were taken a little later on but at least you can see who they were.

Harry and Dad became very close after we were married. They did many building and home repair projects together. He learned a lot from my dad, in fact, Harry once said that he was the dad he never had.

Mom and Dad always had their door and arms wide open, ready to help us in anyway they could. Being newlyweds and then a little later having Joey and Ricky, seems we were always calling them for advice. I honestly don't know how we could have got along in those early days without them. It would have been a lot harder I can say that for sure.

Speaking of Joey and Ricky, Mom and Dad adored them and all their grandchildren.

Many times, they would just call, "We're coming over to pick up the boys for the day." Of course, that day would almost always turn into an overnight. I always made sure I packed their 'Jammies'.

Joe and Rick loved spending time with their grandparents as much as my parents loved spending time with them.

Joe, Rick and I will always miss them, till we meet again.

Thank you, God, for those precious times and memories!

MY DAD'S BAPTISM

My Dad accepted the Lord just before he began to get sick.

Harry and I with the kids attended their church on occasion and on this Sunday, we were there for his Baptism.

For some reason or general procedure of the church, the Pastor instructed Dad to sit up front and the rest of the family to sit behind him.

We all did as the Pastor asked. Then, Harry looked around and said to me, "I'm not leaving dad sitting up there by himself!" Then went and sat with him.

"Thank you, Harry, for sitting with my Dad."

A few months later, my Dad passed. Joey was five, Ricky was three. Harry was devastated.

He had never in his life lost anyone that he was so close to.

They both had love and respect for each other as a father and son.

Following that, Harry supposedly had a 'nervous breakdown' and was admitted to the hospital. (A day or two later his diagnosis was changed to Severe Hypo-Glycemic Reaction which still required several days in the hospital.)

It was during that crisis that Harry's own father, Paul came and stayed with the babies and I.

He said to me, "Honey, I can't pay your bills but I can see that there is food on your table."

He stayed with us until Harry came home from the hospital and got on his feet and back to work.

"Thank you, Paul, for helping out our young family!"

"Thank you, our precious Lord and Savior for bringing such good men into our lives"

CHAPTER 2

YOUNG FAMILY LIFE

OUR FIRST HOME

We were thrilled when our Duplex became available shortly after the Tornado.

A few months later our first baby son was born.

We named him after his father, Joseph Harry Glavosek, Jr. He was such a happy little guy and we were proud new parents.

Fortunately for us my parents lived nearby and were anxious to help with the baby and give moral support to us new parents when needed. (Which was a lot of the time.)

I was able to be a full-time stay-at-home mommy. Harry didn't want me to have to work outside of the home, as he felt it his duty to support his family. He remembered how his mom worked all of the time and wasn't able to be home much. He didn't want that for his Children.

Two years later we had another son whom we named Richard Michael Glavosek. He too was such a good little guy. We were so blessed to have two Healthy and Happy little guys. 'Ricky' was born 1 week before 'Joey's' 2nd. Birthday.

Joey and Ricky grew up being best of friends as they were so close in age.

They had many fun play times and adventures. Both boys were happy, adventuresome and busy little guys.

They certainly kept Mommy and Daddy busy. Life was great and we were full of awe!

Harry with Joey and our Dog, Cindy

After about 3 years we were outgrowing our 2-bedroom duplex, having 2 little busy boys. It was time to go to the next chapter.

We had been saving for some time to buy our first home and found it in North Olmsted, Ohio.

I remember sitting in our car in the street looking at the for-sale sign and told Harry, I don't know how were going to do it, but let's try and get this house.

We somehow through the grace of God were able to buy our first home.

It felt like a castle to us. It was only a 3-bedroom 1 bath house, but it had a nice safe yard for the kids to play and a full basement to be able to play in on those cold Wintery days.

It had a detached garage for us to park our car and store our yard tools. Wow! Who ever heard of that?

We weren't able to park the car in there for too long as the tools and outside toys began filling it up.

It was somewhat of a fixer upper for sure, but we were young and full of energy. We loved where we lived, it was perfect in every way, at least for a while. We got to know and become friends with some of our neighbors whom I still keep in touch with to this day.

We usually stayed up late night after night, after the babies were in bed, painting and working on projects, sometimes well after midnight.

The next day Harry would head off to work on time. When he came home, we would pick up where we left off the night before. That included week-ends until our home was done to our satisfaction.

He was a young man and self-taught himself home improvement and repairs. He became a Mr. Fixit and problem solver. I do believe he passed that trait on to his sons.

Through the bitter cold northern winters, our basement became a wonderful place for our little boys to play.

From Hot Wheels and Big Wheels to an assortment of toys, it was a good place for them to run, like little boys do when they can't play outside.

We eventually set up our basement as our family room.

We had my dad's Pool Table down there as well as the Bar my Dad built us.

Later we attained an old Wurlitzer Juke Box that played all the old rock and roll music on 45 records. We bought it for $75 from my Cousin Bob who worked for a vending company. $75! Boy if we had it today, what it would be worth.

We loved to have friends over on the week-ends and threw lots of fun parties. Many good times were spent with friends, neighbors and family in that house.

When there was a family event, usually it was held there. When my brother Ken married Ruth, Harry's sister, their reception was held there.

Harry was a hard worker but he also loved to have fun and live life to the fullest. 'Work hard, Play hard was his motto.' 'We need to Enjoy Life, the Life God has blessed us with each and every day'.

HIS MUSIC AND TECHNOLOGY

When we first married, he purchased an Accordion from a Minister that played it at his church.

Harry didn't know how to read music and played by ear. He taught himself to play that Accordion!

He generally played every day when getting home from work. Said it helped him relax from his day.

Some years later he bought himself a 'Fun Machine' where he learned many new songs.

However, it wasn't too long before he wanted something bigger so he bought himself a small organ and soon was playing some songs all the way through on that.

While he was learning he tended to play a song over and over so much that I think the whole family still remember some of his songs like 'I'm forever blowing bubbles'.

His love for music continued throughout our time together. He continued to learn more and reach for new technologies.

A few years later at our home in Peachtree City, he traded that organ in on a big Lowery Organ with foot pedals, bench the works. It was amazing with all the woofers and tweeters. He would play for hours.

Sometimes on a Saturday morning when he thought the teenagers in the family had slept long enough, he would play songs and turn up the volume until it rattled the windows. Of course, I got a kick out of it, but not sure if Joe, Rick or Paula enjoyed it. They never complained, but if they did, they kept it to themselves.

I kept that Organ for many years after he Passed, hoping someone in the family wanted to learn to play. But it just sat there looking lonely and needing to be played. It was so large (two sets of keys and tons of buttons and switches) that it probably wouldn't fit in anyone's home.

Finally, I was approached by a Church Organist, Judy, to see about letting her Church buy it.

Since it was going to a Church, I let them have our beautiful Organ for $500.00! I think Harry would have been okay that I sold it.

I wish I could have recorded some of the songs he played on that beautiful Organ. I loved to hear him play.

A couple of songs in particular he played so beautifully – 'Let There Be Peace on Earth' and 'Amazing Grace'.

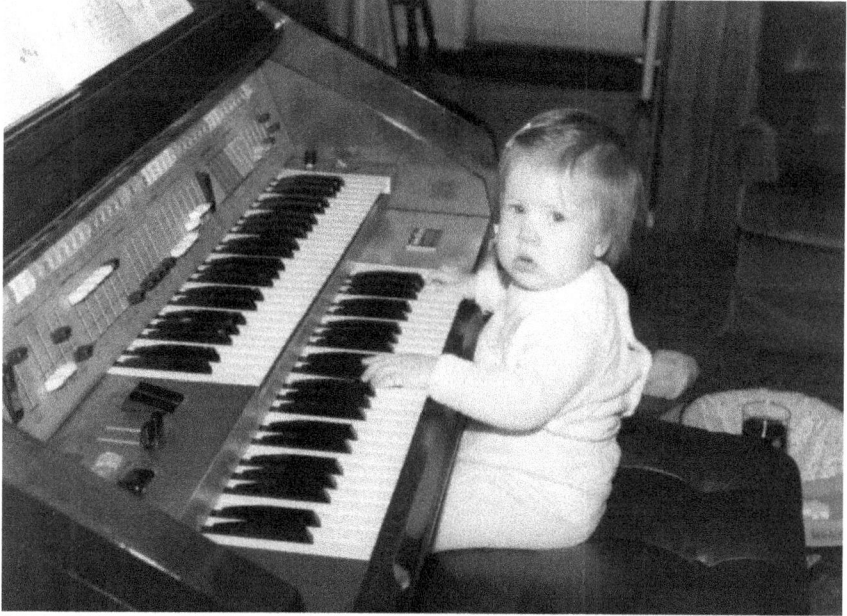
Kira playing on Papa's Organ

He was always on the leading edge of Technology it seems from music to cameras. He loved new ideas. He'd bought a new Sound System to record with tapes and home movies.

We were the first family on the street to have a VHS player. Wow it was as big as the top of our big TV box. No flat TV's yet! The first movie we watched on our TV System was "Superman" in VHS. We had fun with that.

As time went on technology got smarter and smaller. He was also one of the first on our street to get us a big screen Color TV.

It was in a very large cabinet and took up a good portion of the wall in our family room. We had many entertaining family evenings watching movies on that television.

Our Babies loved to watch and listen to Harry play his
Accordion!

CHAPTER 3

PAULA!

While living in our first home in North Olmsted, Ohio. Harry and I talked about having another baby and hopefully it would be a little girl to round out our family.

A few years later, Paula Michelle Glavosek our precious daughter, our blond hair blue eyed little bundle of joy arrived! Our family was now complete. We were thrilled to be a family of five.

She was born with a dislocated hip and had to be in a body cast for a few months, then lots of physical therapy. Before long she was walking and running like any other toddler.

Harry was so thrilled to spoil his little girl; she could do no wrong in her Daddy's eyes. She was daddy's little girl for sure, she was and always will be.

Her brothers also were proud to have a Little Sister!

Her 'Momma' loved dressing up her little girl and doing little girl things.

Later on, I will share how her Dad and I gave her the fairytale Southern Plantation Wedding of her dreams. Nothing was too good for our little girl.

CHAPTER 4

BOATING AND CAMPING

This deserves its own chapter as well as it was a big part of our Family's life together. We were the typical young family living the American dream.

During the week he would go to work and I was lucky to be a stay-at-home Mom and Housewife. I guess if it were up to me things would have stayed the same, but my husband never let grass grow under his feet, he was always thinking of some new adventure to explore.

It was during those days in Ohio, Harry decided our little family needed a Boat. I had never even been in a boat except once and that was my girlfriend's parents cabin cruiser. Plus, I was afraid of deep water and wasn't a very good swimmer, so I was not exactly excited about the idea of a boat. He convinced me it would be good family fun.

As it turned out it was a lot of fun but not right away. That took some doing on his part. We lived near Lake Erie, which can get very choppy at times.

Our first boat was a 16-foot Wooden Cruiser Inc. with wooden bench seats, not the most comfortable seating arrangements for sure. The closest boat launch was on the Rocky River near the mouth of Lake Erie.

Well, on several occasions, Harry hooked up the boat and off we went to the boat launch. I would put the little ones in their life jackets while he launched the boat.

Once all aboard, we headed up the river.

Then getting near the mouth of the River, I could see white caps out on the Lake and start to cry! "Please take us back. I don't want to go out there!" and proceeded to put the Babies in their bulky life jackets into the bow area of the boat!

Harry never pushed or argued. He very patiently turned the boat around, took us back and loaded the boat back on the trailer and headed home.

I don't know how many times that happened but it was several times. Harry never complained, not even once. With that said it did help build up my confidence on the water as I trusted my Captain and we did have many years of boating fun.

Our next boat was much more comfortable!
18-foot StarCraft

Eventually he was able to enjoy fishing on Lake Erie with his buddy's Ray Russ or Roger Carson.

Talk about a fresh Lake Erie Perch dinner when they got home. Nothing better!!!

After he had a great day of fishing, we teamed up. He cleaned and I cooked them! That worked for us!

It wasn't too long before he sold that little wooden boat for a bigger and more comfortable boat. Our new 18ft StarCraft with its deep V haul made a much smoother ride.

Of course, one thing leads to another and it wasn't long before we started Camping on weekends and exploring the inland lakes. The Children and I eventually learned to swim as I felt a whole lot safer than being on Lake Erie.

Our Truck/Camper towing our Boat
Our Suzuki Motorcycle on the front Ramp Harry built himself.

We traveled with our 'Rig' many week-ends, with all our toys. We both loved to travel and did as much as possible.

Paula, Ricky and Joey with Dad in our New StarCraft!

CAMPING

Just about every week-end we packed up the little ones and off we would go to the lake, weather permitting, sometimes even when weather wasn't permitting.

We started out with a Tent, but with the cold Northern nights many times we would wake up freezing cold!

Harry would have to get up in the middle of the night to relight the Coleman Heater.

We loved our Tent Camping Trips but soon discovered the limitations of it.

He was always thinking of making his family and himself more comfortable which brought up the idea of a Camper! It wasn't long before he bought one.

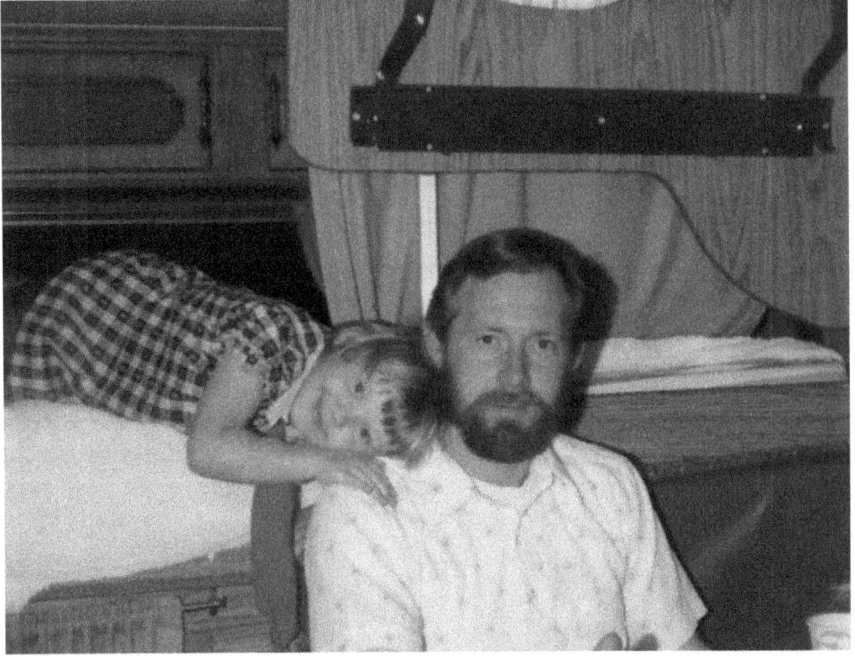

A little story about how we were able to buy our new camper.

Harry and Ray Russ were coming back home from a fishing trip on Lake Erie. They'd driven through Cleveland and were passing by a Camper Sales lot when Harry spotted a Camper sitting lopsided on its bottom. Apparently, the jacks hadn't held or were not properly stabilized. (It was at this Camper Dealership they just happened to be going by. At least that's what he told me. like sure!)

Anyway, the Salesman told them if they could move it that day, he could have it for a real 'unheard of' price'.

It was a brand-new slide in truck camper. Well, he bought it and yes, he did get it up on the truck. He never told me how he did it but Ray told me I really didn't want to know. I am sure he used a tire jack or two, glad I didn't watch that.

That's how Harry rolled, he thought on his feet and figured things out to get the job done whatever that might entail.

After that we enjoyed many more camping trips and felt like we were in the lap of luxury. Our new camper had a bathroom with sink, toilet and shower, gas stove, refrigerator, nice kitchen sink, heating and air-condition and it slept six!

He took the Camper to work with him, and fixed the Jack problem by adding more steel reinforcements. We had no further problems and used our little camper for many years.

It was during those fun filled week-end camping trips that he taught himself to water ski, which meant I had to drive the boat towing a skier. By that time though I loved boating almost as much as he did.

He taught all the kids how to ski as well, they trusted their Dad and did what he instructed them to do. The boys I am sure remember, but somehow, he would take one of them out with him, get on the skis while holding a child, then once we took off, he would ask Ricky or Joey or Paula whichever one was with him to step down on each ski one foot at a time while he was bending over to help them reach the skis. That's how he taught his kids to ski. They are all good water skiers today because of their Dad. I think all those fun-filled times camping and boating gave our children the love of the great outdoors.

There were some Sundays we found little country Churches to attend. One Sunday we found a little church having a revival in the woods and they asked us to join them, so we did. We sat on logs that were set all over for the revival. What a wonderful experience that was worshipping God in the woods surrounded by nature.

PAUL

During that same period of time an event occurred in our young family life. Harry's father Paul.

As I mentioned Harry was very much a family man by heart and helped his Mom, Dad, Brothers and his Sister when they needed him.

Rick, Harry, Paul and Paula, Joe

One day his Dad had really hit rock bottom and called Harry for help. Harry picked him up and brought him home to live with us for a while so he could get on his feet. He made Harry a promise that he would never take a drink again if he helped him.

Paul kept that promise as we never saw him take a drink again, to my knowledge he never did.

He got a good job as a mechanic and was able in a short time to get his own apartment. He stayed in touch with us and our kiddos as well. Later on, our Grandchildren got to know their Grandpa Paul!

Thank You God for helping Paul keep that promise!

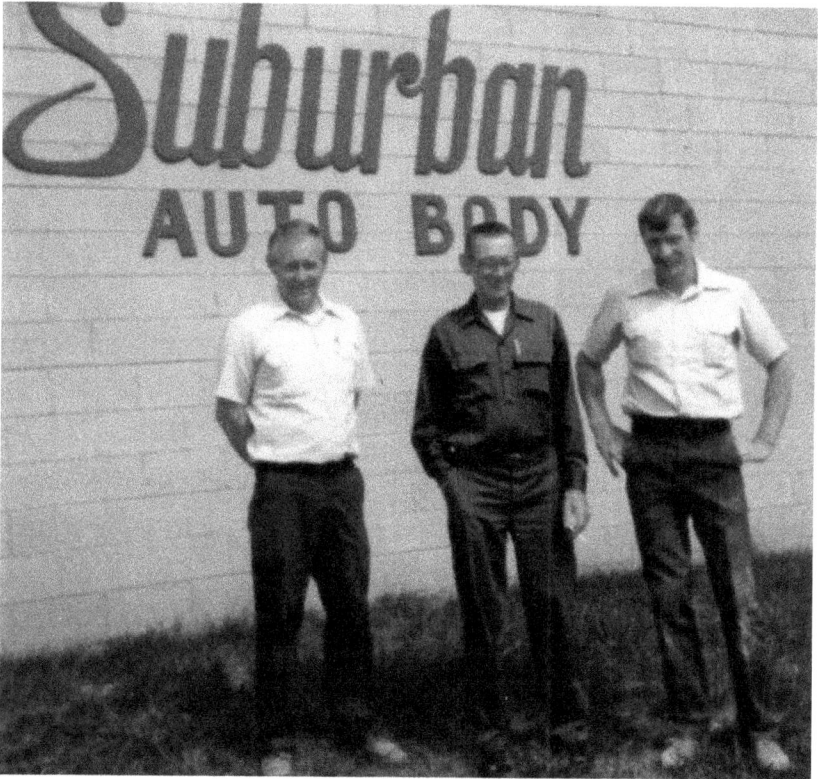

Harry, Paul, and Tom Glavosek

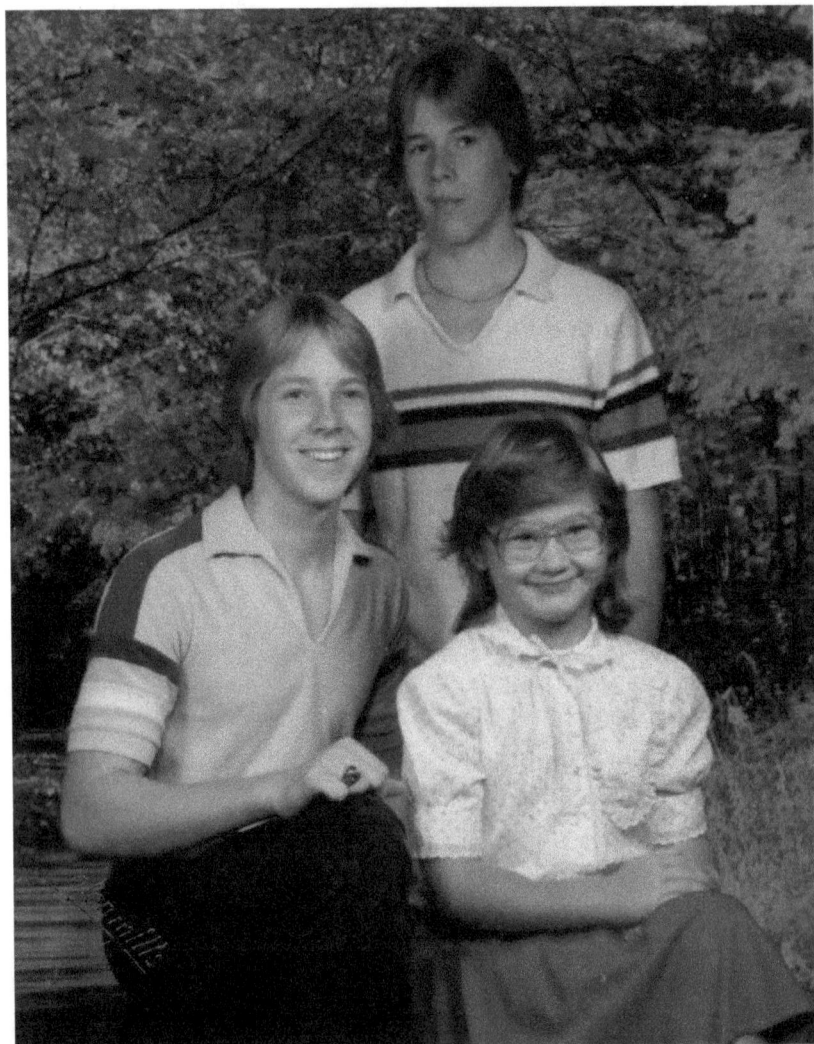

Joe, Rick and Paula 1982

Our Portrait in 1982

CHAPTER 5

MOVING TO GEORGIA:

It was Spring, at Easter Vacation ('Spring Break') when we decided to load up our Rig and take a trip to Georgia.

We wanted to go somewhere nice and warm. Why we picked Georgia as a destination I really cannot say (except looking back now it must have been divine intervention.) We camped at Lake Altoona, just north of Atlanta.

It was then and there that we fell in love with Georgia. It was so warm we had to buy some new clothes as we were packed for cooler weather. It was ok because wearing shorts and boating in April was new to us. We loved it.

After our holiday, we came back to Ohio to face and deal with a heavy snow on May 2nd!

It was that day Harry said to me, "What do you think about moving to Georgia?"

I answered, "Okay."

We were both up for a new adventure.

We both were sick and tired of dealing with snow.

For him, the snow-covered roads, getting to and from work, keeping our driveway shoveled, and waiting for the snow plows to clear the roadways.

For me, I used to drive the boys to the end of the street about ½ mile and have them wait for the school bus to stay warm in the car.

One day I drove back home with Baby Paula and the car just slid off the driveway into the middle of our yard!

On top of that, Baby Paula and I had to walk to the bus stop to meet the boys after school, wait, then walk back home. Brrrrr!

It was hard to deal with that daily I had to admit.

Guess what Harry had to do when he got home from work in the dark and cold? (Winter days in Ohio are very short!)

Both my folks had passed away a few years earlier, so we thought 'What's keeping us?'

Harry had a good trade by then as both a Body man/Painter and had some history as a body shop manager.

Joey, Ricky and Paula were all still little people, so the timing seemed perfect.

Well, we sold our house in Mentor, Ohio one week after listing it!

Harry quickly gave notice at work.

Two weeks later he left the company with some very good references...... Let the Adventure begin!

We loaded our Camper and packed for a week or two as we had no idea where we would land.

Where we were moving depended on where Harry could find work.

We first traveled and searched Tennessee, then South Carolina then Georgia. Our first goal was to locate possible employment, then investigate the housing situation.

We depended on newspapers and in person visits at Dealerships with Body Shops.

This was back in 1974, so things were a lot different than today. No internet searches.

Harry, being in the Auto Body repair field didn't have a hard time finding a good job. He was hired as Bodyshop Manager at Andy Lewis Chevrolet, a dealership in Fairburn, Georgia.

Then we set out to look at homes in the area. He saw a sign saying Peachtree City and thought we should go check it out as we both thought it was a city like we were used to in Oho. We were in for a huge surprise.

Peachtree City was a planned community with many bike/golfcart paths, lakes, swimming pools, tennis courts and golf courses!

Wow, what was not to love! We found a realtor who showed us houses for several days. Eventually we settled on our 4 bedroom, 2 ½ bath with full basement and 'whole house air-conditioning', a rarity where we came from, and all for less than we'd sold our Ohio home for. My goodness, life was good.

Our Beautiful Home in Peachtree City, Georgia

We were both on cloud nine to say the least. We went back to Ohio, closed on our home, and packed up the U-Haul. Some of the guys in our family helped us get loaded and my brother Ken volunteered to drive the U-Haul for us to Georgia.

Harry drove the truck/camper, towing the boat. I drove the car. Off we went on a new adventure of our lives. Turns out that adventure did change our lives as well as many of our family's lives.

Harry and Judy with Ken Albright

Ken used to say that we were the Pioneers in the family. I suppose we really were. It was all so new and an exciting adventure.

Our First Swimming Pool! We were in heaven!

That first summer we felt like we were on vacation constantly. We rode our bikes on the bike paths, went to one of 3 community pools every day or so. In addition, we still did our camping and boating on the week-ends usually at different local lakes. Wow, talk about the good life.

Harry Slalom Skiing

At the lake where we lived, Lake Peachtree, sometimes after work he would get a hankering to water ski.

We would take the boat basically to the end of our street and hit the lake for a few hours.

As it turned out, we had created a very nice vacation spot for family and friends from Ohio. We had lots of company and loved every moment of their visits. We had a big house and lots of room. We have always loved to entertain. Our home was always open for company. The more the better!

Thank You God for leading us to Georgia!

Another of many stories of how God works: One Christmas back in the early 1970s, as most good parents are, we wanted to give our children the best Christmas we could afford (We always set a budget) and to make them happy on Christmas morning.

I started out by giving the children a copy of the Christmas Catalog from Sears and J.C. Penney usually in November. I told them to circle whatever they wanted and to put a star by the one they wanted most.

They loved dreaming and looking through the catalogs. They knew Santa couldn't get them everything, so they only circled the most important things and put stars by the ones they wanted the most. Remember this was way before the internet. Then after a time I would look at what they had circled and then proceeded to rule out some things and try to fill the others.

I called in the order, then when the gift came in, I went to the store to pick it up. (Didn't have home shipping yet!)

Joey wanted the Charlie McCarthy Ventriloquist Dummy which I was able to find, however Ricky wanted the Willie Talk Ventriloquist Dummy which was nowhere to be found. I suppose it was a very popular toy back then.

I called everywhere and looked in every store near us, even put my name on a backorder list at the two catalog stores should one come in. Basically, I searched high and low and made many phone calls around to no avail.

Then, Christmas Eve was here and still no Willie Talk. I was in the kitchen making dinner and talking to God as sometimes I do while working, I asked him to please help Ricky to have a wonderful Christmas and not be too disappointed that he didn't get Willie Talk.

I turned it over to God to take care of the situation.

Harry had to work that day at the body shop in Newnan

When he got off work, he passed by Johnson's Hardware Store and had a thought, what if?

They were just getting ready to close, but the nice owner let him in just before he shut off the lights.

Well low and behold there sat Willie Talk up on the shelf!

When Harry arrived home, he was beaming from ear to ear, then when he and I were alone he whispered in my ear, "Guess what's in the truck??"

I couldn't believe it; it was 'Willie Talk'! I cried happy tears with excitement.

Wow, you see God loves all the little Children and answered this Momma's prayer. Needless to say, the Children, Mom and Dad had a very blessed Christmas!

CHAPTER 6

OUR EXTENDED FAMILY

Tela, our first Foreign Exchange Student

Sometime back in the late 70's we received a flyer in the mail saying there was a need for Host Family's for foreign exchange students. As if our family wasn't rich enough with our three, we thought it would be a really good experience for our children to learn about other Cultures and meet other students.

Through the foreign exchange program, the students could speak English and were required to speak our language daily and learn about our customs.

In 1977 we met a beautiful and a bit shy girl from Columbia, South America. All 5 of us went to the airport to greet and welcome her to Georgia and our home.

Her name is Luz Estella, or 'Tela'.

She was a bit shy at first but soon became such a joy to have in our family. She only lived with us for 6 months but became family. We still keep in touch after all these years.

Her father and mother from Columbia visited us once during her stay. Tela had many brothers and sisters.

Tela with Ricky and Joey

It wasn't too long before Tela was just like a daughter to Harry and I. She was a sweet Teenager and a little older than the kids.

We took her on several camping trips and that summer we planned a trip to Washington D.C. and then continued on to Ohio to meet more of our family, Aunts, Uncles and Cousins.

Judy, Harry, Tela and Paula at the Lincoln Memorial.

All six of us traveled and stayed in the camper for two weeks on our way to Washington D.C. visiting many interesting places and historical sites along the way. It was a fun trip.

To the most
beautiful family
I've ever known.

Love ya!

Tela

Jan. 27/78

While Tela was with us she attended Fayette County High School and was preparing for College when she got back home in Columbia.

What happy memories we made together as a family. Getting closer to time for her to head home, her parents asked us if her brother Puyo could come and stay with us too, as he will be attending the University of Florida and needed to immerse himself into the English language before he could attend there.

Of course, we said yes. I think there was about a 2 week overlap when Puyo came and Tela left for home. He too was shy at first, but before long became one of the family

Tela's Brother, Puyo Came six months later.

The two of them showed me how to cook Plantains among other Columbian dishes. They also brought us gifts from Columbia which I still have today.

After Puyo's stay was nearing the end, we also had another Martelo brother, Milo stay with us for six months for the same reason. During this time, he also became like a son to us.

FAMILY STYLE--The Glavosek family in Peachtree City has expanded in recent months. Mr. and Mrs. J.H. Glavosek and their three children have shared their home for the past six months with Tela Martelo (second from right), a foreign exchange student from Colombia. Her brother, Puyo, (right) has now arrived to take her place and will attend Fayette County High School this fall. Shown with their mother, Judy, are from left, Joey, Ricky and Paula Glavosek.

Both Puyo' and Milo were very good looking and had no problem attracting the ladies! Harry would let them borrow our car for dates.

To this day many years later I still consider them Family. They are very special people indeed.

Harry and I did the best we could to make their stay educational, fun and enjoyable. It was a really wonderful and memorable few years I am sure none of us will ever forget.

Both Melo and Puyo taught my boys some Spanish, some not to be repeated. Boys being boys.

Puyo, Rick, a Columbian friend, Paula, Milo, Joey

All three Kids have continued on in Life to be wonderful people, some with Families of their own.

CHAPTER 7

FAMILY MOVING TO GEORGIA

Harry, Ruth, Mike and Randy Glavosek

One by one each of Harry's brothers and sister as well as Harry's mom eventually moved to Georgia. After vacationing with us they too began to love it here.

First Tom & Carole and their children Tommy, Timmy and Tammy. Following them, Mike, Gail and their children Sandy, Sherry, Rachel and Chrissy. Then came Randy & Laurie and their son Jack.

My brother Ken, Ruth & their kids Tony, Daniel and David spent many vacations here over the years and finally moved down to Georgia following his retirement from the Cleveland Police Dept.

Marie, Harry's Mom, with Me and Harry

Harry's mom Marie moved down to Georgia and remained for some time. The kids got to know their grandma very well.

It wasn't until after Harry passed that Paul, Harry's dad came to live in Georgia.

That primarily was due to Harry's son's Rick and Joe talking their Grandpa into moving south and actually helping him move.

Ohio winters are quite cold and Paul had several health issues and now needed nursing care.

The timing was good in that most of his family lived here and saw him through his final days.

Harry, Paul, Ricky and Joey

It was during that time that he accepted Jesus Christ as his Savior.

"Thank you, God, for letting Grandpa Paul's grandchildren and great grandchildren get to know him and witness to him. They never knew him when he was drinking as he had promised Harry many years before that he would stop drinking and his grandchildren would never see him take a drink. He kept that promise."

Talk about a Ripple Effect, Harry and I never knew what changes would occur in other family members lives because of our decision to move from Ohio to Georgia. Changing so many lives, I believe it was for the better. Some evidence.......

My brother Ken and Ruth's Anniversary with Family

CHAPTER 8

THE BODY SHOP DAYS

Harry hated working for someone else, telling him what to do and when to do it. He wanted to be independent.

Throughout his young life however, many people had told him that he would never amount to anything.

Harry knew better and never let that stop him or get into his way of his thinking. He had other ideas and always dreamed of being his own boss.

He'd also been told time and again that he could never have a business of his own.

No matter, Harry paid no attention to people trying to put him down. He knew they were simply trying to save him grief and just pushed that much harder to achieve his dreams.

Then one day his Dream did come true.

After lots of hard work and planning he and I opened up our own Body Shop and Wrecker Service in Peachtree City.

That Business became one of the most successful in the State of Georgia!

Suburban Auto Body
Peachtree City, Georgia

Several Insurance adjusters said that we were the largest independent body shop on the south side of Atlanta.

He very quickly bought our first two wreckers, a Standard Tow Truck and a little later a Flatbed wrecker.

'Little Red' and 'Big Flat Bed', our wreckers

Our son Joe drew and painted all the Lettering on the trucks as he was quite skilled at that. Later on, he did the lettering for Peachtree City Police Vehicles.

Soon Harry lined up work with the Peachtree City Police Department to help out when and wherever they needed us, night or day, seven days a week. So began our Wrecker Service and night call outs!

He also helped the police or fire department as needed. For instance, on one occasion, he put a car in the lake so they could practice underwater rescues.

He was always doing things like that for them. He was a great friend to the Police Officers and Firemen in Peachtree City, Georgia.

That was the 1980s. Yes, he did it against all odds, Harry may have only gone formally to the 8th grade as he had to get out and support himself to survive early on in his life. I guess you could say he went to the school of hard knocks.

Yes, he was a survivor because he had a positive outlook and choose to never look at the negative no matter what his situation was. He knew God had his back; he was never afraid of hard work to make things happen. He also knew that things just didn't happen because he Prayed about it, that it was up to him to take action to make things happen.

He was told 'never' go into business with your wife. Obviously, he did not listen to that.

He worked hard on setting the stage and contacting lots of folks, getting the word out with the insurance companies, police and fire departments in Peachtree City.

He contacted local citizens, attended City meetings, and submitted newspaper adds. (no internet back in those days) He was Networking long before it became a well-known term.

We took out a Small Business Loan, bought property and had our first shop built. Later, he became friends with Jerry Crozier, our Banker who helped secure our loan.

I jumped in feet first to help my husband. I had no clue about running a shop, in fact I was terrified. Up to that point I had been a stay-at-home mom except for a few seasonal jobs.

I really didn't feel qualified to handle such a big task, but I was a quick learner and Harry helped me along the way.

Harry wrote the estimates, ordered parts, repaired and painted the cars and worked with the customers. I kept the books, paid the bills, learned quickly how to do payroll, quarterly and yearly taxes, and handled lots of paper work. (Computers were not available.)

I kept the office clean and sometimes helped in the shop as needed. I also washed cars or picked up client's cars. We were covered up most of the time with work right off the bat, which meant we immediately had to hire body men right away.

In two years, we'd outgrown our location at 127 Huddleston Drive and moved to a larger facility at 313 Dividend Drive still in Peachtree City.

Oh boy, I remember the day he took me to see the property on Dividend. He was so excited he could hardly contain himself. It was a huge facility with big Bay Doors, a very large shop area for parking, the front had a very large front office with several other offices down the hall, with his and her restrooms, plus the property was already fenced.

All I could think of is how in the world could we afford this? He said "Let me worry about that, I haven't let you down, yet have I?" Like I said Harry dreamed big and went after his dreams.

We hadn't yet listed our property on Huddleston when   in walked someone asking to buy it......   Sold! Word travels fast in a small town.

Before we knew it, Suburban Auto Body had moved to this huge shop on Dividend Drive.

Harry was quick to obtain the proper equipment needed for the new shop.

We purchased a state-of-the-art Paint Booth complete with forced fresh air and a paint mixing system to help get the exact color match. A short time later, we had the Alignment Equipment installed as well as a Car Lift. We didn't want to sub out work like in the old shop and needed the right equipment to speed up those quick turnarounds.

I seemed to stay in a state of worry as he was always upgrading. However, that turned out to be good thing as he was making things happen faster and better than before.

Fortunately, we stayed covered up with work and seemed to always be in need of more Body Men or Painters.

We eventually hired Teens to wash cars and clean the shop, however, those Teens many times didn't show up. And, of course, I had to keep a pair of jeans and tennis shoes in my desk to help wash cars and do their duties.

Our Kids helped as much as they could after school. After Graduation from High School, they worked full time.

The whole operation was very time consuming for us all. However, despite the hard work, there were perks to owning our own business.

'WORK HARD. PLAY HARD'

Although we took many planned Family Vacations and weekend Camping Trips, sometimes he would do things spontaneously.

This one particular time I remember he surprised me for our 20th wedding anniversary a Cruise to the Bahamas.

We had never done anything like that before, but with the busy shop and all he thought it was time we take a time out for ourselves.

68

He'd gone to the local travel agency and bought our tickets and it wasn't long after, we drove down to Port Canaveral to board the ship.

It was a wonderful time. We sailed on the Big Red Boat, which now is of course repurposed I think for dinner cruises or a casino as the newer ships are much bigger.

At any rate we had a wonderful time, even went to the casino and pulled a few slots. Didn't win anything but we had fun!

We had not experienced anything like this before and of course, the meals were out of this world.

I've been hooked on cruising ever since.

ANOTHER SURPRISE

Because Suburban was so time consuming for both of us, it seemed that on week-ends or our days off I would be busy trying to clean up our home.

Harry suggested that we hire maid service once a week to take care of that. I never would have thought of that, so thankfully we did use a service for a few years.

That sure helped free up my time with more time for Harry and I to do fun things. Thank you, Harry, for that.

Our shop was a family-owned business, as he wanted it to be.

Joe and Rick learned the trade inside and out while they were in High School.

Their father was a perfectionist as they soon learned to be. He taught them all he knew about the auto body repair business.

Our nephew David worked in the shop as well and today is a very successful auto body repairman making a good living.

Joe and Rick both drove very nice cars, but they worked hard for them. Harry and the boys would buy wrecked cars from an auto auction and bring them back to the shop to rebuild them.

Harry would let the boys and some of their friends he knew and trusted work on their own cars over the week-ends. He told them "You're not to have any party's here and as long as the shop is ready for work Monday morning, I have no problem."

They always left the shop clean and ready for business Monday morning. We had no complaints in that regard.

Paula, when not in school, also worked in the office primarily as my Assistant.

Through honesty, hard work and doing excellent jobs for our customers, we acquired a very good name for ourselves.

We were continually growing as Harry and the boys were always improving with new ideas and using the latest tooling and technologies.

Before he was diagnosed with his Terminal Illness, he was once again in the process of expanding our business to a 24-hour Heavy Semi Truck Service.

Had he lived a little longer, I could see at one time or another all of his grandkids would be hanging around the shop a lot, especially the boys.

Possibly someone in the family may have been running it or even owning it today! We will never know.

Suburban Auto Wrecker Service was a 24-hour service.

Harry, Joe and Rick took turns being on call each night. Back in those days they had pagers or beepers as cell phones were not available yet. When their beeper would go off, they called the Police Department for details. Sometimes the police department would call directly to their home phone.

JOE

Two of Joe's wrecker stories:

The first story…

He was on night duty and had a call to pick up a car pulled over due to a DUI.

When he got there the girl that was driving the car was being arrested for driving while intoxicated.

While he was hooking up her car as she was being put in the police car she started crying out to Joe – "Joe please help me, help me Joe". He thought what can I do, so he said a quick prayer for her as she was being arrested.

The second story…

This time he was driving the flat bed transporting a car on the truck and towing another behind.

As he made the turn off Hwy. 74 onto Kelly drive the one in the back broke loose. All he could think of is oh "no, not on Hwy. 74" which was a very busy road.

Suddenly it veered off the road right into the Fire Department sign. It tore up their sign, but he was able to retrieve the car from the fire department lot and get them both back to the shop. Thankfully no one got hurt.

RICK

The airplane crash:

On this particular night it was Ricks turn.

He received a call regarding an airplane crash just off Hwy 85 in Senoia by the river and could we retrieve it and take it to Falcon field.

For a job like this, he promptly called his dad to assist.

At the time, Senoia didn't have a full time Police department and had turned it over to Peachtree City.

Peachtree City Police then called us I believe because they knew Harry and Suburban could and would get this unusual job done.

Well, we had never retrieved an airplane before but why not give it a shot.

He and Rick decided to take both wreckers to the scene as they had to determine what they were up against. (One wrecker was a flat bed and the other was a regular wrecker.) They both loved challenges and this was definitely one of those times.

The aircraft to Rick's disappointment, turned out to be the same Piper Arrow Rick had flown during his flight training. He had taken several cross-country trips in that aircraft. He had considered it as his own plane and was saddened to see the wreckage.

Fortunately, the pilot and his passengers were able to walk away unharmed. They actually could see the runway when coming in for the landing, but ran out of fuel just short of final. They clipped the power lines and landed in the tree tops with the limbs breaking their fall. The plane and passengers had made it safely to the ground. The wings weren't broken off however the aircraft was totaled.

Apparently, they were flying back from somewhere in Florida and thought they would have enough fuel to make it back. Bad mistake and judgment on that pilot, he should have erred over on the cautious side and made a fuel stop!

That mistake could have cost him his life as well as his passengers. He was lucky. The plane not so much.

Somehow Harry and Rick got the plane loaded onto the Flatbed after much maneuvering. However, they ended up having to jack it around somewhat catty cornered for the wings to clear the electrical poles on the roads.

Peachtree City Police worked the scene and blocked the road ways for us.

I'm sure it was exciting and challenging for all to watch Rick and Harry retrieve that plane.

Everything went smoothly Thank Goodness. They dropped off the plane or what was left of it on the ramp at Falcon Field.

The aircraft was a total loss.

Those are just a couple of the many wrecker stories.

I at times had to drive one of the wreckers to an accident scene if Harry needed another wrecker and Joe & Rick were not available. I wasn't crazy about doing that but a wife does what she has to do at times to help. To me they were big trucks with stick shifts and could be intimidating!

Thank you, God, for keeping my guys safe during their days as Wrecker Drivers.

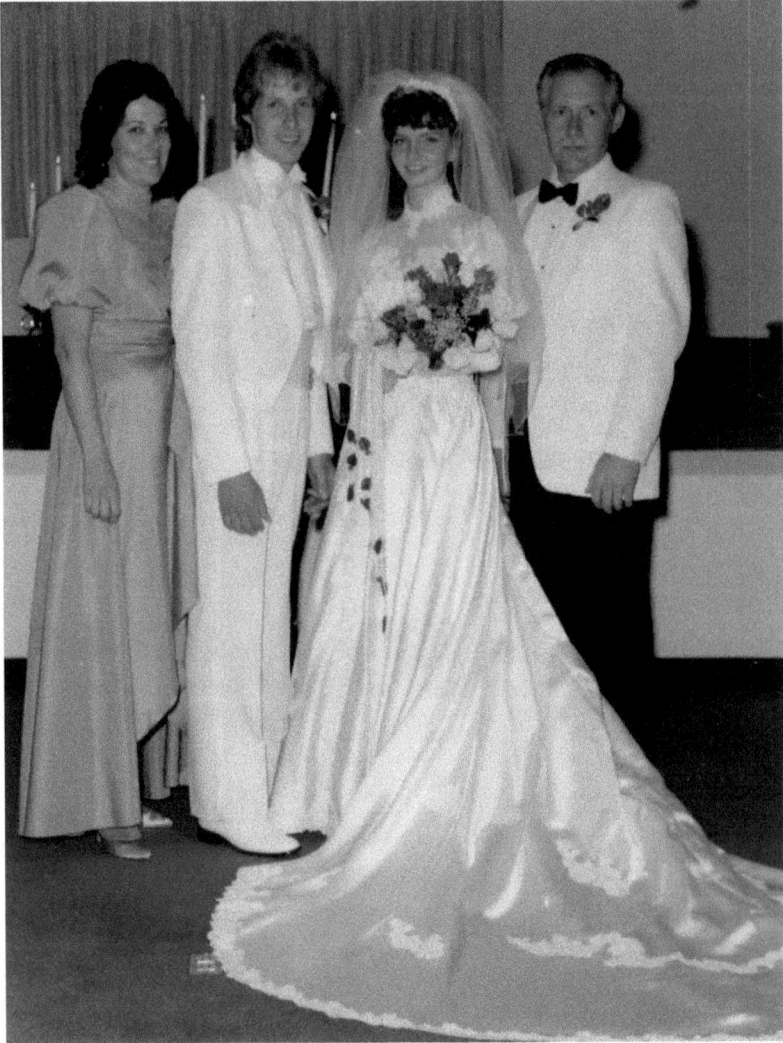

Joe and Jennifer's Wedding with Mom and Dad
Harps Crossing Baptist Church

CHAPTER 9

MARRIAGES OF OUR CHILDREN

It was during the time we owned Suburban Auto Body that each of our kids married, one by one.

First was Joe who met and soon married Jennifer Souza. Jennifer is the Daughter of Jack and Sandy Souza.

It was a beautiful wedding held at their church, Harps Crossing Baptist in Fayetteville, Georgia.

We were both so happy for the new couple and to add a wonderful new Daughter to our family!

They were excited to start their new life together as man and wife.

The Newlyweds took a week-long Honeymoon to the beautiful beaches on the Florida Gulf Coast.

The beach to this day is still one of the places Joe and Jen love to get to as often as possible. Both have a love for travel.

Richard and Kirsten Glavosek with Dad and Mom
Holy Trinity Church

It sure seemed like a short time later for me but it was three years later!

Rick met and married Kirsten Saylor.
Kirsten is the daughter of Barry and Doris McWilliams

They too had a beautiful wedding, this time held at our church, Holy Trinity in Peachtree City.

We both were very happy to welcome yet another beautiful Daughter into our family! We loved that our Family was growing larger each year!

They happily started their life together taking a week-long Honeymoon in St. Croix.

Of course, they too loved to travel.

Soon after each of our kids were married, we sold the smaller Boat along with the Camper and bought a beautiful Cabin Cruiser.

We kept our boat at Burnt Village Marina (now Southern Harbor Marina) on the Alabama side of West Point Lake.

We had a nice slip on 'D' Dock, made lots of friends and had a lot of really good times.

The Kids were always invited and frequently came down for a great day of boating.

Harry and I spent some great days and many nights together on the water.

Our Last Boat – Our Cabin Cruiser!

It wasn't long after those events that we received a surprise announcement!

In the summer of 1986, Harry, myself, Rick, Marty Gray (Rick's good buddy) Paula and Melissa Kay (Paula's best friend) were spending the week-end enjoying Lake Eufaula, Alabama.

We often traveled with the kids and their friends which was great fun for everyone.

We were staying at the Lodge and happened to be in our room when Joe called us all excited!

He exclaimed he was going to be a Daddy, that he and Jennifer were expecting!

Wow! ... We were going to be Grandparents!

We both were so excited! I for one couldn't wait to go shopping for a baby again.

Kira Nicole Glavosek with Papa

CHAPTER 10

KIRA

Kira is the one Grandchild he really got to know.

She was little Miss-can-do-nothing-wrong in his eyes, just like his little Paula.

This was the type of man he was. For example...

One day he picked Kira up from the Nursery while her parents, Joe and Jen were at work.

For some reason Joe, Jen or myself could not pick her up at the day care, so Papa went. Well, when he came to the front door, he heard his little granddaughter crying her eyes out.

That did not set well with him at all.

When the lady finally came to the door to let him in, he was not very happy to see that Kira, standing in her playpen was still in her pajamas, had a soggy diaper and was sobbing her little eyes out.

She had tear stained cheeks and was trying to catch her breath from crying so long.

When she saw her papa, she jumped into his arms from the playpen.

He held her tight as he picked up her things to leave then asked the lady how much was owed her. She said that Joe & Jen would pay her. He then said "No! You do not understand. She will not be coming back. How much do I owe you?

He paid her and that was that. So, from that day on twice a week baby Kira stayed with me at the body shop office.

Of course, sometimes when her papa had an errand to go on, he took his little Kira with him. She adored him and he adored her!

One time he had to take one of the wreckers somewhere and took her with him. He put her car seat in the truck and off they went on their little outing. She would go anywhere with him.

Although all the kids were welcome to spend the day on the lake with us, Kira was the only one invited to stay overnight.

She spent many nights in our Cabin Cruiser with us. Papa even played Barbies with her. The things Grandfathers do for their first-born grandchild.

Had he lived, I am sure each and every Grandchild would have a similar story about their Papa. He would have loved them all. Somehow, I believe he does love each and every one and is a very proud 'Papa' in Heaven.

86

Joe, Jen and Kira enjoying the Cabin Cruiser

~

Harry did meet one more Grandbaby before he Passed, Kira's Sister, one week old little Baby Katelyn.

He only managed to give her a Kiss on her cheek, He was too weak to hold her or I know he would have.

I wish I could have taken a picture of that. I'm sorry I couldn't but that little sweet Kiss will always be instilled in my memory.

Kira, Harry, Ruth, Mike and Randy

CHAPTER 11

ONE YEAR PRIOR

Several big events happened a year before he Passed.

Harry suffered a Heart Attack and had to undergo open heart surgery.

He was towing a friend's boat for him and while he was driving, kept holding his chest and taking deep breaths.

I kept asking him if he was okay, he kept telling me he was fine. I was starting to get worried as I had never seen him like that. Keep in mind this was all the while he was driving the truck.

I kept asking him to please let's stop at the LaGrange hospital just to be safe, he wouldn't hear of it and drove us on home. We arrived a good hour later.

He immediately went upstairs and laid down on the bed, still holding his chest. By that time, I was really getting worried and was going to call 911 but he heard me and yelled for me not to.

Why did I listen? I can't answer that, I just wish I had not listened to him. Don't ever listen to someone if you think they are having a heart attack. Call 911.

Thankfully Joe, Rick and Kirsten came over and talked some sense into him. He then allowed us to drive him to the hospital. He would not go in an ambulance.

Joe drove us in our car. Rick & Kirsten followed in theirs. When we got to the Fayette Hospital it was confirmed, Yes, he was having a heart attack.

They immediately put him in ICU and did what they could for him, but they told us he really needs to be transported to Piedmont Atlanta where they are equipped to handle this situation.

He of course balked at the idea, then in walked our friend Jim Sherril who told him not to be so stubborn.

He finally agreed to be transported to Atlanta.

Joe, Rick and I followed the ambulance to Atlanta. Turns out one of his main artery's was completely blocked. They tried to do a Balloon Angioplasty on the Coronary Artery but the artery kept closing up.

The doctor explained to us what was going on and that Harry needed to get to surgery as soon as possible to have a Coronary Artery Bypass.

All seemed to go well as he recovered rather quickly from the surgery. Soon he was back home and we were out walking a couple of miles every day.

He was determined to walk our Daughter Down the Aisle. It was just six weeks until Paula and Jeff's upcoming wedding.

As you can see, his determination paid off.

PAULA AND JEFF SCOTT WEDDING WITH OUR GROWING FAMILY

Windemere Plantation

Jeff Scott is the son of Jim and Linda Scott.

We rented the Windemere Plantation near Fairburn, Georgia for the week-end. Harry hired a band, rented a Dance Floor, a huge Tent for 150 guests, a full course hot catered meal, and a Wet Bar! You get the picture. It was his gift to his little girl.

Because we had the tent, tables and chairs already it was decided we would have the Rehearsal at the Plantation as well as the Rehearsal Dinner.

He spared no expense, even had to rent white chairs because he thought they would look better for the Wedding plus we bought real silverware for over 150 people! (Still have some of the wedding silverware today.)

At our request the caterer used glass plates and glasses. The cost in today's dollars would be hard to guess, but that wedding cost us over $10,000 dollars and back in those days that was a lot of money, still is a lot of money.

He wanted to go wedding dress shopping with Paula and I. Not only that he was hands on planning her and Jeff's wedding and even made the bouquets for her Bridesmaids.

Let's just say that he had his hand in all the arrangements of the wedding large and small from the Music, Flowers and everything that goes with planning a wedding. Nothing was too good for his little Daughter. He even interviewed Bands!

His six weeks of Walking and Dogged Determination had paid off. He was proud to walk Paula down the aisle and even danced the Father – Daughter Dance with her!

CHAPTER 12

LAST DAYS

BAPTISM

Around the time he first got sick he had been reading his Bible about Baptism, especially the scriptures regarding 'by Immersion in Baptism.' *John 3:23, Matthew 3:16 and Acts 8:38.*

Although he had been Baptized as a baby in the Catholic Church and knew he was a believer and going to Heaven, he felt he needed to do more.

He had become friends with the Pastor that performed the Ceremony for our daughter Paula and son-in-law Jeff's Wedding. He was the Pastor of the Peachtree City Christian Church.

We were worshiping at Holy Trinity Catholic Church at the time and occasionally attended his Church as well.

After talking and getting to know more about the Church and him we were considering joining his Church.

Well, he asked Pastor Bob Tyler if he would baptize him and of course he said yes. That following week, March 17, 1990, Harry, myself, Paula, Joe, Rick & Kirsten were all Baptized by Immersion at the Peachtree City Christian Church.

At that private Service, We all

Renewed our Faith and accepted Jesus Christ as our Personal Savior

Al, my brother, came down to help Harry move the boat 1990.
Al, Joe, Rick and Harry

JUDY:

This is going to be one of the hardest things for me to write, but I believe it must be written. It may help another person, even if only one, that's going through something horrific in their lives.

I want you to know that you are never alone, *He* is always with you, even when you do not feel *His* presence that does not mean that *He* is not with you, trust me *He* is. So, with that said here's goes my story as best I can to share with you.

Harry and I were in our late 40s, had been married 25 years now, our children were all grown. Joe our oldest was happily married, Rick our middle child was happily married and our daughter Paula was also happily married.

So, now we were Empty Nesters and thought we may be able to do more traveling, something we both loved.

98

We had a very successful family business, Suburban Auto Body and Wrecker Service in Peachtree City, Georgia. We had nice home also in Peachtree City and each of us drove a nice paid for car and truck, plus we had a Cabin Cruiser we kept at Lake West Point. We as a family worked together plus we loved to play at the lake together. We were and still are a very close family. We were living the American Dream, life was good. That was all to change for us, bad things happen to good people. Our whole life as we knew it was about to be turned upside down in a blink.

We never know what lays ahead of us, so for that very reason we should most definitely live each moment as if it were our last and enjoy our family and friends more and try not to worry about the what ifs and daily problems. Problems will always be there in some form or fashion. People may not.

MATTHEW 18:20

For where two or three are gathered together in my name,
there am I in the midst of them.

After his Heart Attack and surgery, what had seemed at the time like an eternity, his Doctor finally came to us and said that he was in recovery and had suffered some heart damage.

However, he also said to expect a full recovery with proper diet and exercise which he could begin after some healing.

He did heal and was out of the hospital in about a week. From there, we began walking every day. He was on his way to a full recovery.

Six weeks later he did walk our daughter down the aisle and on top of that, had the dance with his daughter at one of the most beautiful Southern weddings I have ever seen.

It was a hot that day in June 30, 1990 and of course I was worried that he may have over done it, but he was having none of my worries on this very special day. When I think about it, I think Paula and Jeff's wedding was as much for Daddy as it was for them.

Thank you, God, for giving us this day of joy to celebrate the Union of two very special people and the joy that it gave Harry to be able to do this for our daughter and son-in-law. I know that if it were not for your healing hands this would not have been possible. Thank you, Father.

I wish I could say that we lived happily ever after but that was not meant to be.

So, this journey of life continues.

In August 1990 Harry had a real sharp pain in his chest while we were on one of our walks. I thought maybe he was having another heart attack, but he assured me it was not feeling like it had before. We immediately went home and scheduled a visit to the doctor just to have Harry checked, they did an EKG and it showed nothing and he was feeling fine. The doctor told us possibly it was his chest bone healing still from his open-heart surgery he had in May.

We went home and thought nothing more of it. Harry felt fine.

By the fall of that year Harry was starting to feel sluggish, tired easy and was just not himself. Wanted to walk less and rest more. So, we tried to take it a little easier and not push so hard with our daily walks.

We had endless details of the business and home, everyday stuff trying to get 'stuff done' things. Rick and Joe took over managing the affairs of body shop more so their Dad could take it easier. I found myself carrying my briefcase where ever I went since I was taking care of the books, paying the bills and making payroll. I had to keep up with that. Bills do not care what you are going through, they demand to get paid regardless of your circumstances.

The customers, estimates, parts, employees, job details and insurance matters were all handled by our sons. So, for a while that seemed to be our norm. Harry of course would go to the shop just about every day for a short while to look in on things. He didn't really know how or really want to take it easy. Unfortunately, his body told him otherwise, so he would rest.

We got through Christmas and Harry was still not feeling better, in fact he was feeling weaker and short of breath. In January 1991 we paid his cardiologist a visit and they ran more tests. They were not liking the results of the tests and had him admitted to the hospital for more tests. Something was going on in his heart but they could not figure out what and decided they had to go in for exploratory surgery.

Well, they scheduled the surgery for the very next day. We alerted all the family and friends to cover him in prayers. Joe and Rick got the shop covered so they were at the hospital with me during the surgery.

What seemed like eternity, how many hours I couldn't say. To this day I am so Thank-full to God for making sure I was not alone at this horrible time. I had my sons by my side. When we finally saw the doctor coming down the hall toward us, he had his head hung low. I instantly thought that Harry had died, and felt like I was going to faint. I found myself going down when both my sons held me up and caught me.

The doctor ushered the three of us into a Family room to discuss the results. He assured me that Harry did not die, and was in recovery. What he told us next was just unimaginable and very hard to process. They had found a tumor inside his heart. They had taken out what they could and sent it to the lab for testing, but being in the heart they could not remove it all. He then told us they will do all they can for him with Chemo. However, the outcome didn't look good, unless we wanted to be put on an organ list for a new heart.

It turned out he had an extremely aggressive Melanoma of the Left Ventricle. In fact, the doctor told us they had never heard of Heart Cancer before and after research only found two other cases in the world.

The doctor then told us we could go back in recovery and see him, but warned us to please not share with him their findings until he could be there to monitor him. So, the boys and I went back to see Harry. His poor body was pale and very swollen from the surgery. As soon as he saw us walk in, he lifted both hands with thumbs up! Indicating he made it through ok! It was all I could do to keep my composure and had to step out to regain it. Thankfully God gave me the strength to do so. I am sure it was equally hard for Joe and Rick. We hugged him and told him reassuring comments. I held tightly onto his hand.

Finally, which seemed like forever our Cardiologist came in, along with an Oncologist to tell him their findings, and discuss a treatment plan and what we might expect in the very near future. Harry's blood pressure shot up and an alarm on his monitor went off. The doctor quickly was able to give him something to calm him down. Harry very quickly regained his composure and asked the doctors well what next? What are my options? We all then prayed together along with our two doctors.

His only option was chemo or a heart transplant, he opted for Chemo as he said he did not want to be opened up again!

During that long hospital recovery period. I stayed with him night and day until he could come home.

He continued the Chemo treatments for several months.

OUR LAST TRIP TOGETHER:

It was during the time in between going to receive Chemo treatments he said to me that he would like to go on a trip, just the two of us. He thought he was up to doing it in between treatments and that we both needed a change of scenery. We talked to Joe and Rick and they said no worries, they would take care of everything at the shop, no problem.

We packed up the Blazer he and the boys had recently rebuilt and just coming out of the shop, he felt it needed to be driven. Plus he didn't want to pile more miles on our new Toyota.

The Blazer was one of the cars Harry had recently bought from a salvage auction. He and the boys did that often, buy salvage autos, sometimes as many as a couple a month and rebuild them to like new condition.

The Blazer did fine, all except for the first 100 miles or so as pieces of glass would blow out of the vents. Finally that stopped.

He wanted to drive all the way to Key West, down one coast and back up the other, with no particular time frame.

We did that trip in February 1991. He did most of the driving going down.

We left the sun roof open most of the trip once we got to Florida to breathe in and enjoy the sea air. We picked tomatoes, strawberries and blue berries in Southern Florida and enjoyed eating them in our hotel room.

The drive to Key West was so beautiful, crystal clear aqua blue water on both sides of the roads and bridges. We took our time and stopped to take a few slow long walks on some of the beaches along the way, resting a lot in between.

Once we got to our hotel in Key West, we enjoyed a tasty seafood lunch at the famous landmark 'Captain Tony's'.

Later on we had Key Lime Pie and coffee at yet another famous landmark 'Sloppy Joe's'.

From there we drove around a bit, taking in the sights and sounds of the island before heading back to our hotel.

It was a bittersweet trip; we both tried our best to keep our spirits up because we both knew it would be the last trip we will ever take together as man and wife on this earth.

Being in the warm sunshine was a huge boost to us both. We did a lot of praying, soul searching, talking and asking God to please help guide us on this journey we were facing. We both needed some quiet time together, just the two of us, with no distractions.

We were so afraid for each other and worried about what we each were going through. The trip gave us the time to really talk a lot, but mostly being in the safety of each other's company.

He lost most of his hair on that trip and started wearing a ball cap to keep from getting burned.

By the time we got to Key West he was really getting more tired each day. We spent a lot of time in the hotel room.

We decided it best to not return back by the East coast of Florida, but just return home the way we came, which was the West Coast, but not to stop too much.

We left Key West and drove until he was too tired to go on and stopped at the nearest hotel for the night. The next day I started doing all the driving.

We stayed the next night on Sanibel Island on the Gulf Coast where we'd stayed with the kids a few years back. He said for 'old times sake'.

From there I drove straight home, stopping only when necessary. He slept comfortably most of the way home with his seat reclined. It was a very quiet and somber ride home.

By the time we got back home we felt somewhat ready to face the next chapter in our lives, with God, family and good friends walking beside us with each day.

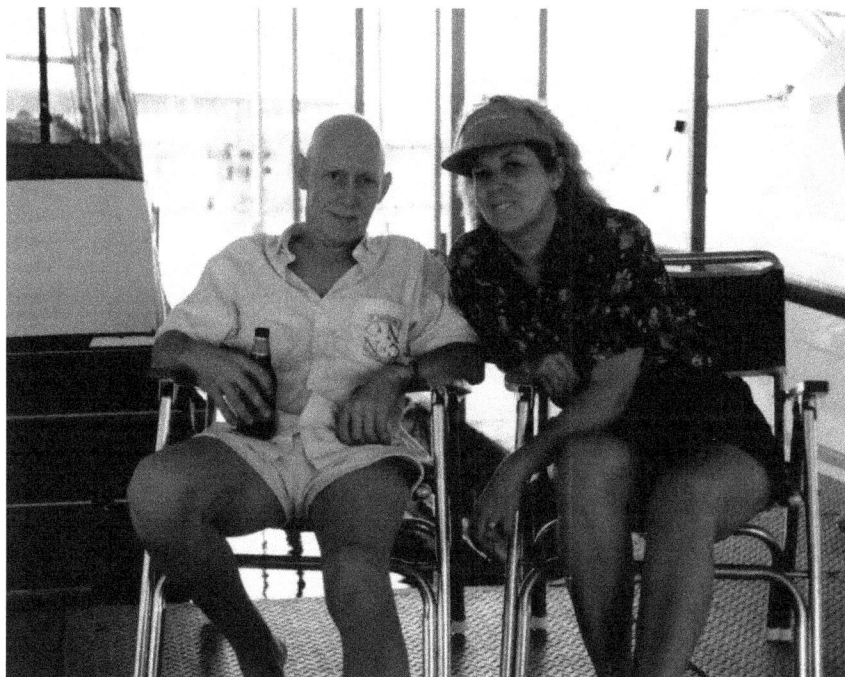

In June 1991 just between both of our birthdays he decided he would like to go down to the boat one more time and spend the night.

I was extremely skeptical however and worried as his health had really deteriorated at that point.

I was taking him every two weeks to the pulmonary doctor to get the fluid off his lungs so he could breathe better. This in itself was a huge concern for me, but he pressed on and won. Afterall how could I refuse to take him to his boat one more time. Anything to make him happy, I was just concerned for his welfare.

I drove us down to the Marina at Lake West Point a little over an hour away to spend the night on our boat.

I was really hoping that some of our boat friends would be there but this was a weekday and the docks were pretty empty.

We took the boat out for another run soon after we got there. Later I grilled some fish and veggies for dinner and we had a nice evening. He commented he almost felt normal.

We had a relatively good night's sleep. However, come early morning he was beginning to feel very tired and sick so we knew we had to head home asap.

Here is where the scary part comes in, getting him off the cabin cruiser onto the dock safely.

I held on to him the best I could and got him to the swim platform and onto the dock to sit on a chair I'd placed there earlier. I really wanted to get help but he insisted no help needed.

Oh, how I prayed for God to please send someone to help me get him to our car without falling into the lake. We were on a floating dock so there was some movement.

While he waited there, I pulled the car down along a steep embankment and parked as close to the water and dock as safely as possible.

I'd just opened the passenger door when suddenly I knew my prayer had been answered.

Two men from over on the houseboat dock saw what was going on and immediately came over to help. They didn't ask if we needed help, they just helped!

"Thank you, God, for sending those kind men to help us, also for letting him spend a little more time on his boat! I know you were watching over us!"

VERY LAST DAYS:

Harry had a positive attitude about things. He had a way of taking lemons and making lemonade.

Even at the time of his last journey of life, being told he has an aggressive form of cancer in his heart which had no cure. He held his family together with his attitude and faith to accept what was dealt him. He was not afraid of dying as he knew where he was going, to heaven to be with Jesus. His biggest concern was leaving us, his family.

We also held onto the hope that where there is life there is hope. Again, for his family he did go through the horrible treatments of chemo for months, until it became evident it was doing no good. The cancer was still growing. He wanted to be the best he could be even near the end of his life; he was a very strong man with courage of steel, a man of deep Faith.

He never asked why me, he would say why not me. He did try and make light of it sometimes I think for our sake. Once he said it would have been more fun to have won the lottery, which was for sure the truth, it would have!

He was always thinking of how he could help me through this hard time the best he could. He set out and got his things in order.

We had a good friend, Jim Sherrill who happened to be an Attorney. Harry asked him if he would write up a quick claim deed, putting everything in my name, the house, car, truck, Bodyshop, wreckers and equipment, everything. That way I wouldn't have to worry about all those details later.

Bless his heart, he then told me after all the papers were signed "Honey you can throw me out on my ear now that I don't own anything!" I didn't find that the least bit funny. That was Harry though trying to bring some laughter into a heavy and heartbreaking situation.

Another thing happened during his last summer. I still can not believe the timing. We got a phone call from Westminster Gardens Cemetery, seems they were having a 'buy one, get one free' special on Burial plots, including the Vaults. I really thought it was a very sick joke, due to our circumstance and the timing.

Turns out it wasn't a joke and they knew nothing about us or our current situation for that matter.

He asked them if we took the offer could one of the plots be used in the next few weeks/months, and explained to them his condition. They said yes of course.

I'm standing there, my mouth open in shock, I couldn't believe the conversation he was having with a Sales Person from the cemetery!

He said, "We'll buy them, can't afford to pass up that deal." Later, Paula and I went to the Cemetery to pick the Plots and sign the Papers. In retro spec I know this had to have been very hard for him to do, but he never showed it.

When the time came our Doctors could do no more, they referred us to Hospice. Harry told me he would go on to the Hospice Home so he wouldn't be a burden to me.

Well needless to say I would not hear of that. He would be staying home with me and that was final! I had to be his guardian angle and look after him.

The first day the Hospice Nurse arrived at our home, Harry wasn't home! She couldn't believe it. She assumed she would find him in bed.

But no, he was still driving his truck over to the body shop to check on things once in a while, although not every day.

However, it wasn't long after she arrived, he drove up.

The Nurse then went over with us what to expect in the next few weeks/months. They wanted to set up his hospital bed in our Livingroom but, well he would not hear of that. He was a very private person and wanted to be in the Master Bedroom upstairs.

After they protested a bit, the two delivery men succumbed to his wishes and managed to get the bed upstairs.

Each day I could see him getting weaker and weaker. At first, he would get up, shower, get dressed and go downstairs for breakfast, before accepting visitors.

Then climbing up the flight of stairs became extremely hard for him and he usually needed help from one of our sons. At that point or soon after he stayed in bed upstairs most days. I kept him as comfortable as possible. I was young, strong and wouldn't allow anyone else to help me when it came to his personal care, except the Hospice Nurse of course.

Family was great, coming over daily to check on us and to take care of any household chores, meals, shopping, etc.

He and all that helped him knew how much he was loved and cared for. He was never a bother to any of us.

When his doctor asked him if he had any wishes before he died, he said yes, I would like to see my Grandson born, our Daughter Paula was pregnant, due in October. Everyone thought she was carrying a boy. (Jeff and Paula later on, had a beautiful baby Girl, Meggan.) He would have been totally happy of course, however that wish was not meant to be granted.

He also wanted to take his sons, Joe and Rick and his son-in-law, Jeff down the Chattahoochee River all the way down to Apalachicola, Florida.

He wanted to experience it again, this time with his sons.

(A few years before he and I had taken our Boat down the Chattahoochee River from Columbus Georgia to Apalachicola Florida and out into the Gulf. We'd traveled through three Locks and traveled about 250 miles or so. It was quite and adventure, I'll never forget.)

It was an awesome trip that he and I were able to do twice, he would have loved to do it one more time with the guys. That wasn't meant to be either.

Looking back on those days I know now that we were Blessed that we had our own business as I was able to stay at home and care of him in our home.

I was thankful that Joe and Rick could and did handle the workings of the business. From home, I could do payroll, pay the bills and any other paper work that needed done.

He never went to Hospice; I would not hear of it.

One little note, he was always a very neat and groomed person. This time in his life was no exception. He did not want any visitors until he was able to get washed and dressed for the day. I had to honor that and sometimes had to ask someone that happened to drop by to visit him to please come back later, Bless their hearts but I had to do that for him. He wanted to be up and dressed and downstairs, (up until the last 2 weeks) before receiving any visitors. That was ok, it was important to him.

During his illness while he was confined at home, he had lots of visitors. That included men from both Holy Trinity Catholic Church and Peachtree City Christian Church who spent private prayer time and fellowship with him. And, many times, men from the Peachtree City Police and Fire department would stop by to see him as well. He had touched so many people in our community and was loved and respected by many.

Most of my brothers and sisters were here from Ohio and were with us the day he went to be with the Lord,

I was alone with him in our room, was praying with my head laying near his chest. I heard his Last Heartbeat. Part of my heart went with him that day, until we meet again. He was now at peace and no longer in pain and could now breathe freely.

What I saw next still astonishes me.

As I sat looking out the window there appeared millions of Beautiful Yellow Butterflies. I felt a huge comfort somehow.

Moments later our three Children were by my side to comfort me and each other.

The rest of the family that were in the house that day gave the four of us time to say our Goodbyes to a very Special Man. Each of us prayed and consoled each other.

I want to Thank God again for sending me Godly family men and women to be with me during those very dark days, especially the days that followed!

"If I hadn't thanked you before I am Thanking you now, God" You knew I so needed them.

Also Thank You to my kids and brothers and sisters for being there for us.

The next few days of planning the funeral are a blur.

I do remember both my son's and brothers went with me to the funeral home to make the arrangement, to even helping me pick out his coffin.

Somehow, I felt like I was in a very bad dream that I couldn't wake up from. Nothing seemed real. I was numb and really couldn't feel anything. When he died a part of me died I guess. Maybe it was God's way of protecting me during those times, making everything not feel real.

One thing I do remember vividly that day as we were driving to the funeral home was one of the brightest and most beautiful rainbows I had ever seen. It seemed to illuminate our car.

I felt comfort in the Rainbow as I knew Harry was in the arms of Jesus. I know it was a sign from heaven, assuring me everything would be alright.

He went to be with our Lord on Aug. 30, 1991

Joseph Harry Glavosek
Westminster Memorial Gardens
Peachtree City, Georgia

Joseph Harry Glavosek was Survived by his Wife Judy, Joe (our son) and Jen (our daughter-in-law), Their two little girls (our granddaughters) Kira and Katelyn, Rick (our son) and Kirsten (our daughter-in-law), Jeff (our son-in-law) and Paula Scott (our daughter, Pregnant with Meggan).

His Funeral was held at Holy Trinity Church in Peachtree City.

I was completely surprised and amazed when we arrived at the Church.

As we drove in, I noticed the parking lot was totally filled.

Lined up with the Funeral Procession were Police and Fire Department cars as far as I could see. The Officers were in their dress uniforms. Wow I was shocked as I had not expected that.

When I entered the church, I still could not believe my eyes. This very large church was packed full! All the Pews were filled and people were standing all along the side aisles.

I felt overwhelmed with love. I didn't know my husband had touched that many people's lives and was loved by so many.

One of the men from our church, Jim Stagg sent me a package after the Funeral containing a Letter and Poem he had written about Harry along with some notes from his Service. I've included both later in this section.

For myself, Harry was a kind, fun-loving man who loved God and his family dearly, in that order.

He was a Christian man who loved our Lord and studied the Bible from cover to cover. He was always interested in Bible Prophecy. He quoted scripture often, sometimes to make a point.

When we were not working at the shop, (which was most of the time for quite a few years) the family loved to take off to the lake, camping, boating, fishing, skiing or go to the Florida rent a condo for a week, or make a trip or two to Ohio to visit family there (which was a least once a year). We loved to travel whenever we possibly could.

I feel blessed to have been a big part of his Life. We were husband and wife yes, but we also were also best of friends.

I would never trade those 26 years with him. I feel that Joe, Rick and Paula and I are all much better people having known him and loved him. We were very Blessed indeed.

I would never have missed the Dance I had with him.

If you get a chance to sit it out or dance, I hope
You Will Dance!

The Letter Jim wrote to me along with the Poem:

"Dear Judy,

I hope you, the family and especially Paula are doing okay. I would have stopped by, but I just had throat surgery and thought it best to mail this to you instead.

In separate envelopes are two items which I wish to give to you for keepsakes for Harry's memory. They are in envelopes because if you do not wish to keep them you do not have to look at them, just throw away. My aim is not to bring more hurt to you, but to offer you some small remembrance of Harry that I had.

The large brown envelope contains a copy of the reading from scripture which we did at the funeral and my homily notes.

The small white envelope has a poem which I wrote for Harry, and I was going to give it to him before I went into the hospital but never made it. Then after he died, I added the last verse and I was going to give it to you, but I couldn't work up the courage to do it at the wake or funeral. The words reflect the impact Harry had on my life, and will continue to have every time I think of him. These items are not very valuable except that to his family. They represent the respect and the love I had for him. He was my friend and I'll always be proud to have known him.

Even though you have received a great loss, your strong faith and strong family gathered around you will remind you that Harry left you and the family a great legacy --- he left people behind who will remember him for being a good and kind man --- - I don't think any of us could wish for more.

I stand by ready to help with anything I can for you and the kids. Please call me when I can help.

Much love – Many Prayers, Jim Stagg"

Man of Faith

Man, of faith, your actions speak
Louder than all sermons heard.
We watch you strive; we watch you seek
To serve the Lord, to serve His Word.

Man, of faith, an attitude of peace
You show to us who are afraid
Of worldly costs that stress our souls,
So, we may hope such strife will cease.

Man, of faith, your trust in God
Amazes us who call you friend.
We ask our Lord that we one day,
With faith like yours, can face our end.

From Jim to Harry, August 16, 1991-

Man, of faith, now you sleep
In Christ's own peace, your life here done.
Please pray for us, who here still stay,
To build our faith in God's own Son.

Jim Stagg

-Epilogue, August 30, 1991-

JIM STAGG, DEACON, HOLY TRINITY CHURCH

Dedicated to

Harry Glavosek – August 30, 1991

On Friday afternoon, when Judy, Paula and Marlene and I reviewed the many scripture readings which could be used today, we looked for reading that reflected Harry Glavosek's outlook on life.....and on death.

These readings today all contain a strong message of hope, not unrealistic wishes for improbable events, but a calm, thoughtful, mature trust in God, as well as in people, that characterized Harry.

Maybe today we don't talk about hope as much as we do the other theological virtues of faith and charity. It's as if it were the unimportant of the three, and yet its placement in the trilogy – Faith – Hope and Charity – is significant. Hope is the glue that holds faith and charity together. It is the flowering of our Faith into a complete trust in whatever God has in mind for us, and that trust allows us to Love God, through life and even through death and into eternal life with HIM.

The words from the book of Wisdom touch close to home for us today.

"The just man, though he dies early shall be at rest."

We know in our hearts that we are at rest only when we put ourselves into the hands of God. Now many of us fight this idea every day. We want to be our own person. We want to do things our own way. Sometimes we are the ones the writer says "saw, and did not understand."

Psalm 23, so well-known to us all.... a comfort for a hurt mind or soul: "Beside restful waters he leads me, he refreshes my soul."

There are few other words written that describe so well these thoughts that come from absolute trust in God. In truly believing and hoping in his plan for us, and in the ultimate success of that plan.

The message from Revelation and from Jesus' own words in today's gospel inspire not only Faith, but Hope in our Lord's victory over death. That "There shall be No More Death", and his promise that he brings Eternal Life.

For each one of us who was touched by Harry's hope – by his deep trust in God – we have a responsibility to continue his example to us. To pass it on, to build within ourselves a connection between our Faith and our Love of God. To build Hope – Trust – in God who creates us and sons and daughters and grandchildren in his image. In God who redeems us and our friends, and our enemies, with his blood shed on the cross, in God who sanctifies us to live with HIM for endless time.

Jesus, in the gospel today, gives us the grandest hope of our lives, the plan HE and HIS FATHER and The SPIRIT have for us for all eternity:

"I am the resurrection and the life; whoever believes in me, even if he dies, will live, and everyone who lives and believes in me will never die".

In Harry's memory, may we all today answer with Martha, in faith and in love and in great hope:

"Yes, Lord, I believe that you are the Messiah, The Son of God."

PSALM 23:

R). The Lord is my shepherd; there is nothing I shall want.
Though I walk in the valley of darkness, I fear no evil, for you
are with me.

The Lord is my shepherd; I shall not want.
In verdant pastures he gives me repose;
Beside restful waters he leads me;
He refreshes my soul.
He guides me in right paths for his name's sake.
Even though I walk in the dark valley I fear no evil; for you are
at my side
With your rod and your staff that give me courage.
You spread the table before me in the sight of my foes;
You anoint my head with oil; my cup overflows.
Only goodness and kindness follow me all the days of my life;
And I shall dwell in the house of the Lord forever.

CHAPTER 13

LOVE AND REMEMBRANCE

This Chapter was open to everyone who felt compelled to write a little something about their relationship with Harry.

It includes both Friends and Family members as well as words from our South American 'Kids', the Martelo Family.

From this section you will probably see more of the wonderful character of the man and the Christian that he was.

Written by his daughter, Paula Glavosek – Scott - Dec, 2020
Some Memories of my father:

Dad had a way of making everything better. If he said things would be Okay, they were! He had a kind soul and everyone who met him liked him.

He and I would go to the grocery store frequently, just the two of us which I loved. One because it was just, he and I, and another was because he always let me get whatever I wanted, even the expensive cookies that Mom would never buy. Lol!

From the moment we got out of the car someone was always saying "Hi Harry"! Inside the store it continued. I remember this woman said Hi and then just kept on talking and talking, when she finally left, he just smiled at me. I then told him "I'm telling mom you are talking to her!" He just laughed. That's just how he was a very friendly person.

I remember another time we were boating at Lake West Point. Dad loved to explore islands and would dig up plants from old homesteads and replant them in our yard at home. He always carried a small shovel and pail for just those kinds of things. As we were exploring an island one day my brothers were teasing me saying watch out for snakes and laughed. Low and behold I tripped and did get bit. Dad took us back to the marina right away and they told him to get me to the hospital asap. He picked me up and carried me to the truck. I was on top of the world as I was with my dad and he was my hero. By the time they took care of the bite and got the poison out, before we headed back to the marina to get Mom, Joe & Rick, as they had to stay with the boat, Dad asked if I wanted some ice-cream before we got to the marina. Oh yes, I did! I felt I was Dads "Golden Child." It was a good day!!

On my wedding day Dad and I sat in the bride's room at the antebellum home he had rented for the wedding. Just the two of us waiting to walk down the aisle, my father and I. I had a crinoline under my wedding dress, yes, I was a Southern Belle bride, getting my southern plantation wedding of my dreams, given to me by my father! We went to sit down and my hoop went straight up and smacked me in the face. I yelled for dad to help me. Dad was very proper! He wouldn't look at me but reached over and tried to push it down. As he moved it smacked me in the face again. We laughed! Then in the middle of the laughter I told him to look at me. He said I can't I will cry. He then said you know if you want to leave, we can. I won't be upset, I don't care about the money, I care if your happy! I told him I loved him and would always be his baby girl no matter what, but I love Jeff for my husband! We then proceeded him walking me down the aisle as planned!

At the reception I remember very well the father and daughter dance. Dad hugged me and said he loved me and was proud of me. I didn't want that dance to end. I am so proud to be his daughter.

Dad may not be here on this earth but he never leaves me! My daughter Meggan was born a few months after Dad passed. I was so sad he didn't get a chance to see her. I was so wrong. Meggan's bassinet was in our bedroom by our bed. She was asleep when I happened to be walking by the door to check on her and there in the dark sat my Dad on the edge of the bed. He had his hand on Meggans back, he turned looked at me and smiled. I was frozen I cried and turned to tell Jeff and when I looked back, he was gone. There was place on the bed where he sat that was still warm.

He also came to me when I miscarried. I was at my lowest, but dad came to me in a dream! He looked young and he was holding the baby Jeff and I had just lost. He was dressed in a white gown and he told me don't worry about your son he will grow up here with Jesus and me! From that moment even in death dad made everything better.

From all the stories you read I hope you come away with knowing he was and will always be a great man of Faith. The world was a better place because he was in it. He was a Godly man who believes we will all be together again soon someday in Heaven! What a reunion that will be!!

With Love and Remembrance,
Paula

Rick:

Written by his son, Richard Glavosek - Dec, 2020

Some Memories of my father:

My father, Harry Glavosek was my Mentor and my friend. My memories of him were vibrant and full of life. He was the type of person that was never afraid of acting on his dreams and he seemed to make friends wherever he went. When he had an idea, he considered it carefully and set out to make it happen. He never seemed to cower to the "what ifs." I greatly admired those attributes in him.

Interestingly, I never remembered him failing at anything. Although, he shared some things about his life that he considered failures, having some run ins with the law when he was a teenager and opening a small body shop in Ohio with a dishonest partner. I only saw him as a person that had the answers to any problems that arose. Because of that, I always asked for and took his advice on any big decisions, even when the advice was contrary to what I wanted to do.

Some of my earliest memories of my father were while on summer break from school, I spent many days with him at work. We would plan for me to join him the night before and in the morning, my mom would come into my room, wake me up and ask, "are you sure you want to go to work with your dad?" Of course, the answer was yes. In hindsight I can imagine that I was probably more of a hindrance than a help to him, but he would always welcome me tagging along. At the time, I felt like I was really contributing. He would give me jobs to do, sanding fenders, picking up and organizing the tools, helping hold up body panels that he would weld in place and listening to him tell me the do's and don'ts of body work. Every chance I got, I would go to the break room and get chips or candy from the machine. When it was time for lunch, we would find a place in the stall or bay where we were working, clear off a space and eat whatever mom packed in his giant lunch box, or so it seemed giant at the time. Sometimes we would go to a local take-out restaurant for burgers or hotdogs. At the end of the day, I would proudly ride home with him while he recapped what we had accomplished. It was in those times that I learned much more than body work. It was in those times that he was shaping me into the man that I would become.

It seemed like destiny that I would become an auto body technician. When I was in High School, I started working part-time at our family body shop, Suburban Auto Body, after a short time dabbling at a couple of the local restaurants. It was there that I started getting some real experience with auto body repair. My dad, having taught me the trade most of my life, allowed me to take on as much and as complex a job as I felt confident with. It was not long before I was a journeyman and working every aspect of the process, from paint and body to frame and suspension alignment. By the time I was in my Mid-twenties, he put me on as body shop manager.

I enjoyed so many times with my dad, but one in particular stands out above others. It was the day of my sister and brother in-law's wedding. Somehow the keys to my truck were packed in a box with some decorations. When the ceremony was over, my keys along with the decorations left the venue and headed to my parents' house. So, as I was stuck waiting on the keys to return, my dad walked up and jumped in the bed of the truck with me. Since I had the keg of beer, he and I poured a cup and sat there talking about the beautiful ceremony and how fortunate we were to have that opportunity to spend that time together talking.

Not all times were as nice as the times mentioned above. I could certainly be difficult, and he sometimes jumped to conclusions. I remember one time that my friend Marty and I went to a local pasture party. Since the pasture was muddy and I was driving a Pontiac Firebird, we decided to park the car in the lot of a local pizza place, Partners II Pizza. Since my father was well connected in the city, one of the local police officers called him and told him that he noticed my car parked at Partners Pizza and that he had it on good authority that I was at the party drinking beer, a party that they were about to raid. So, my dad decided to pick the car up with our wrecker and bring it home, that way I would not be caught drinking and driving. As it had it, I was not drinking alcohol that day, so you can imagine my surprise when I returned to the lot to find my car missing. The first person I called was my dad. I wanted to tell him that I thought my car had been stolen and ask him what to do next. He very somber and quietly said, I have your car and to come home. When I got home, I was fired up. I thought, how dare him take my car, I am a man now and I paid for that car myself! I thought, he had no business taking that car and I told him so. My heated nature escalated the situation into a full-blown argument. I wound up telling him that I was leaving and was not coming back. I grabbed my keys and started toward the door. He very sternly said, "You're not going anywhere." I thought that I was a man, able to make my own decisions. Maybe that was technically true, in every sense of the law, but as I headed that way, I knew in my heart that leaving would have disrespected a man that I admired and respected above all others. It was at that point that I put my keys down and remained as he had commanded.

Of course, we had up's a down's as father and sons do, but until the day that he died, my dad and I truly shared a special relationship. He would tell me from time to time, that he was sure that he and I would have been buddies had we grown up at the same time of life. I recall many times, as I became older, that he and I would sit and listen to music, have a beer, and discuss the events of the day and times from his past. He introduced me to artists like Clyde McCoy and his Orchestra and Dinah Washington. When he had a Dinah Washington album on, you could tell that he really connected with what she had to say. A passion that he passed on to me. To this day, I still enjoy listening to her music. It always makes me think about my dad. What I would not do to relive those moments...

Rick

133

JOE:

Written by his son, Joseph Glavosek - Dec, 2020
Some Memories of my father:

When mom said she was putting together a book about dad, I thought it was a great idea. So, when she asked me if I could also write something about him, I said sure, I'd be glad to. I always love talking about him.

I was incredibly blessed to have him for a dad. He was a great example to me as I was growing up. He loved God, and shared His word with us all the time. I remember dad sharing scripture with me on the phone even after I was married and had a family of my own.

134

He was also a great example to me by the way he loved mom, and how he loved us kids. He was always there for us and we knew we could always count in him.

There are many examples of him being there for me and for all of us, but there's one in particular. I know everybody in the family has heard the story, but I'll share the short version.

As a ten- or eleven-year-old playing outside, I was dragged by an adult to her house. Because of a conflict I had with her daughter. Once she got me there, she called the police on me. At that age, I didn't know how to process that and I was terrified. I didn't know what was going to happen to me.

But thanks to Rick, who peddled home as fast as he could for help, found mom who then met up with dad. So, as I was sitting there scared as I could be, being questioned by the police. All of sudden there was a pounding at the door. Not a knock, but a pounding.

It was dad to the rescue. To say I was relieved when he got there would be an understatement. I knew I was going to be ok then because dad was there.

There was a time about a year later that we almost lost dad. I was about twelve, and he would usually give me a ride to school then, because it was on the way of where he worked. But this one day for some reason I didn't ride with him, I rode the bus instead.

So, as I was riding to school, we passed a wreck, and somebody said, hey Joe I think that was your dad. I said no, that wasn't him. Then a little while later I was called out of class, and when I walked out into the hall, I saw mom and dad walking toward me.

When I looked at dad, I saw that his face was all bruised up, and then I realized that it was him that had the wreck. He saw my bus go by after it happened, so he wanted to go to the school and let me know that he was ok. We were so thankful that he was.

There was so much that I loved about dad. But one of my favorite things about him, was when we would be watching something funny on tv. His laugh was always so much fun to hear. He'd be entertained by what funny thing was happening on tv, and I'd be totally entertained by his laugh.

Dad had a way with words. If there was something you were going through, he knew what to say to make you feel better. One summer when we were kids, my cousins Mike and Ray came to visit us for the week without their parents.

Well, they ended up getting very homesick. So, I remember dad coming up to our room where we were hanging out and talking to them about it. I don't remember anything he said, but whatever it was, it made them feel better. After he left the room, my cousin said, man your dad sure is a good talker.

I got my love of music from dad. I used to love it when he'd break out his accordion and play "I'm forever blowing bubbles". He later got an electronic keyboard called a fun machine, which is what got me started playing music.

He eventually got a bigger organ that he kept in the living room, which he'd play just about every day. He also found it useful for making sure us kids didn't stay in bed too long. Whenever he'd want to get everyone up, he'd sit down on the organ, crank up the volume, and start playing. It was very effective.

I'd love to hear him play that Organ again. I'd love to just hang out with him. One of the things I wish I would've done, but didn't, happened the day Jen and I got married. It was just a little thing, but it was important, and I should have.

136

We were at the house getting ready for the wedding. Most of our relatives were there, and dad was in the kitchen with some of them. He called me in there and asked me if I wanted to have a toast with him to celebrate my wedding, and I said no.

It wasn't that I didn't want to toast with him. I was just thinking that I needed to keep my head clear for the wedding. But in reality, one drink wouldn't have affected my head at all. Dad was just trying to do something special. If I could go back and do it again, I would definitely take him up on it. I'd say sure dad, that would be awesome.

I enjoy telling my children and grandchildren about him, because they never got to meet him. Except for Kira, she got to spend some special times with him the first four years of her life. He did also get to meet Kate right after she was born, and he gave her a kiss.

I have dreams with dad in them probably three or four times a year. I had one just recently as a matter of fact. And when I do, it's like he's still here, and I'm not surprised to see him. But yet it's really awesome at the same time.

He was a great dad! Not a day goes by that I don't miss him very much. Different things and events have happened in my life over the years. And I've often asked myself, how would dad handle this? He always seemed to know. I'm so very blessed for all the years of having such a wonderful dad.

Joe

KIRA

WRITTEN BY HIS GRANDDAUGHTER
KIRA NICOLE GLAVOSEK
FEBRUARY, 2021

SOME MEMORIES OF MY PAPA

Scientists believe people can remember beginning at around three to three and a half years of age, in particular, events of significance in their past. For me it is not an event but a person, my Papa. Though I knew him at a very young age, I knew him not just as a grandfather, but as my best friend. Out of seven grandchildren, and now six great grandchildren (one on the way also), I was the only grandchild blessed to have known this incredible man. When asked about special times or memories I recall with him, I find myself stumped. Not because I can't recall them but simply because there were many such times. I remember the creaking of the dock at the lake where we went to go spend the night on Papa and Ninny's boat. I remember how refreshing the lake water felt when Papa and I played with my Barbies and he drove them on his remote-control boat. I remember down to the yellow slide on shoes Barbie wore. I remember my Papa best as a feeling of comfort, safety, and unconditional love. I remember dipping my deli swiss cheese (the fancy kind with lots of holes) in the lake before I ate and Papa simply letting me do it even though Ninny was appalled. I remember eating cake before dinner and hearing Papa say when questioned, "Because she wants it." He was my champion from day one! To this day, I will sneak something sweet before dinner and grin to myself knowing Papa probably played a part in the wicked sweet tooth I have. Even at my young three and four years of age, I knew this special man would move mountains for me. He was never too busy to snuggle, to play (usually Barbies) and to laugh with me.

As much as we like to remember wonderful memories, our heart remembers times of sorrow as well. I remember not knowing or understanding why but realizing that my precious Papa was tired and seemed slower than our usual "full speed." I remember when his once gray and white hair became very thin and began to fall out. Naturally, I told him "Papa, I don't like your bald head!" Not offended, he said "Neither do I!" To this day, I have an aversion to baldness. Maybe I simply associate it with loss.

While I remember vividly all of our special times together, I remember too the day my Papa, my best friend, went home to be with Jesus. My mom took a call and went into their bedroom to talk. It was a dark and rainy day and she didn't bother to turn the light on. I could tell by her tone that whatever news she had received was very bad. She sat quietly on her bed in the dark and cried after hanging up and when I went in, she let me know that Papa was no longer with us. I don't remember much after that other than family crying, sad days and a void left by a man larger than life.

I knew Papa as my buddy, my confidant and my playmate but it was in later years as those of us who knew him talked about his time with us that I got to know him even more. As a child, I wasn't fully aware of what it meant to be a Believer but I know now that my Papa truly did. He loved each and every one of us but he loved our Lord first and shone Christ's love to anyone he came in contact with. I know he keeps a close eye on us, seated next to our Savior. He sees every happy moment, every heartbreak and knows as we do, that we will see him again. He is still such a huge part of my life-in my heart and in the legacy he left behind. He is in my dad's quiet, gentle nature, his fierce determination, and his love for the Lord. He is in my uncle's willingness to serve, in his laugh and in his smile. He is in my aunt's goofy, playful nature and strong love for family. He is in my Ninny, his bride, who he knew would be strong enough to love us all and to keep us strong when he had to leave before us. He is in my grandpa's peaceful observant nature and steady love for us all. I even see him in my precious boys-they may not have met him here on Earth but they certainly inherited his compassion for others and loving spirit. I like to think I've got some of him in me too, walking beside me when I feel low and celebrating in life's victories.

Though I had such a short time with Papa, this special and incredible man continues to have a huge impact on my life. I count myself extremely blessed beyond measure to have had the time I did. He will forever be my partner in crime and my best buddy! I hope that I'm even half of who he hoped I'd become...and one day I can ask him in person. Until then, I hope I can shine a light as bright as he did ~

With Love and Remembrance
Kira

KATELYN

Our granddaughter Katelyn, Joe's second Daughter was born a few days before her Papa died. We got the call from Joe that Jen was in labor. Harry told me to go ahead over to the hospital that he would be alright until I got home. I think Rick or Paula came over to be with him while I was gone. So, I got him settled and comfortable and made a very quick trip to the hospital.

Before I left, I remembered to grab the video camera on my way out the door. I got to the hospital just in time to see our 2nd granddaughter born, Katelyn was perfect in every way.

I Took a few video pictures of our brand-new baby girl and her happy and proud mommy and daddy. Then I hurried back home to be with Harry. I couldn't wait to show him the video of our newest addition. He was thrilled and got teary eyed as he watched the film and saw his new granddaughter for the first time.

Later on, Joe & Jen brought her by in person to meet her Papa. He was too weak to hold her but he did give her a kiss on her tiny soft cheek.

Katelyn asked me if she could add a little something to this book as she felt compelled to do so.

I was thrilled that she felt this way so of course I said yes!

TO MY PAPA

Written by his Granddaughter, Katelyn Allyse Glavosek – Pline
December 2020

To My Papa,

For starters I love you! I think so often about you and of the gift you gave me, the one small kiss. How often we receive small kisses from loved ones that tend to go unnoticed. Maybe that's what you thought when you gave me that kiss, that I was too young to know. That kiss though I still remember almost thirty years later. One that I will remember and think on until I see you again.

There have been times where I was upset or angry that I don't have memories of you like others do. Praise the Lord though for HE has helped me see the precious memories I do have. Every time a family member talks of you, I'm given a memory. Such as how much you loved your family, you were an encourager, you stood up for what was right, and how you loved the Lord.

Another memory I hold close is when I first acknowledged that you've met the two children of mine that I have yet to meet. I'm so thankful you were there with the Lord to welcome them. If I could only ask you, are they as precious as I've imagined?

How fun it would have been to introduce you to David. I think you'd be proud of him as my husband. He really is an amazing person. Then as for my kiddos, you would adore them, as well as spoil them I'm sure.

I hope you know how much you are missed and how much I would love to talk with you. Just to hear your voice as we talk over lunch or coffee. One day, until then I will learn what I can of you from others. Did you drink coffee?

I'm thankful you were friends with Grandpa. For if it wasn't for y'alls friendship he may have never known our family. Thankfully though he <u>is</u> our family and what a gift he is to us. What a picture of how the Lord knows all things and has a reason for everything.

One last thing for now, can you be one of the first I hug when it's my time to come home? Then of course another Papa kiss, for old times' sake?

I love you so much Papa! One day I'll say that and get to hear you say it back to me, what a day that will be.

Always,
Kate

Written by Marlene Albright – Barucky
My Memories of Harry, my Brother-in-Law
January 2018

When I think of Harry I immediately think, soft spoken, gentleman, friendly, risk taker, hard worker*, successful, generous**, always on the cutting edge of life. When I would come south for a visit Harry and Judy always made me feel welcome and went out of their way to show me a good time. I have many happy memories of our times together from going to Disney World, to Panama Beach, to Savannah and even to Atlanta to see the play "Annie". Or even just staying at home making homemade, peach ice-cream and talking. I loved talking with Harry, he was down to earth and loved to talk about "end times prophecy" and the soon return of Jesus (We know it's even nearer now, don't we Harry:) One quote from Harry that has stuck with me is when he was so sick with cancer, he did not have a self-pity complex. Instead of saying "Why me?" he said "Why not me?" What a wonderful and brave attitude and what a wonderful legacy he left for his family and friends. If I ever face that kind of situation in my life I want to be just like Harry and say "Why not me?" I am so blessed to have known Harry Glavosek and look forward to seeing him again real soon!

*One night in particular we were leaving in the morning in the camper to spend time in Panama City, Florida. But something was leaking in the motor home (I think it may have been the shower) anyway Harry was working on that for a long time and I never saw him loose his temper or his patience.

**Harry would attend auto auctions and purchase cars which had been totaled. He would meticulously put them back together (maybe better than new) and then re-sell them. Well, I was blessed to be the recipient of two of these beautiful vehicles and I'm quite confident that Harry didn't turn much of a profit from me, that's the kind of man he was.

With Love and Remembrance,
Marlene

MIKE GLAVOSEK

This is a letter written March 2018 about Harry from his younger brother Mike.

Early in life we children were generally together. My earliest remembrance of Harry was his seventh birthday. Mother had a party for him. It was under the first maple tree by the driveway. I don't recall who all was there, but it must have been cousins as our grandparents had no indoor plumbing. We had moved to Grandpa and Grandma Owens in 1951. School friends probably were not there. That would have been 1952.

The next thing I remembered was Mother took us kids to see the movie "The King and I" in 1956 when it was released. The only reason I remember that is because Mom made such a fuss about how Harry cried at the end of the movie!

We all lived with our grandparents for about 5 or 6 years. Our grandfather had several heart attacks while we were there.

In 1957 we (Mom and us 5 kids) moved to Mentor-On-the-Lake, Ohio to a very small house, but we all squeezed in there, doubling up in beds, I guess. I remember it was there that we

148

got our first telephone, we had a party line (which means we shared with others). We boys probably had a lot to do with encouraging others to get a private line. We enjoyed silently picking up the phone to listen to other people's conversations.

Lochtan's Grocery was on the corner of our street. Frank the owner let me help around the store. I would take the empty bottles down to the garage & do other little things around the store. Harry at times would retrieve the bottles I had taken down & bring them up to cash them in for the deposit again. On occasion he would take a soda from the inventory, he introduced me to cream soda. This was way before the big chain stores came in like Pick N Pay, 7 Eleven, Lawsons or Kroger. If it weren't for Mr. Lochtans kindness, we would have been a lot worse off than we were. He knew about the pilgrimed but never said a word. At our young age we didn't realize people kept track of their inventory.

Harry was as handsome as a boy as he was a man. I had a little friend, Sarah Ann Holt, that lived just around the corner. One day I went looking for her at her home. Her mother told me that she and Harry were playing in the shed in their backyard. I went home mad at Harry for taking my little girlfriend. That was short lived as we were young boys and had other things to do and think of besides girls.

At the end of our street was a marsh, some of the neighborhood kids would build a raft to ride around the marsh. Harry and some of his friends decided to build a boat. Somehow, they scrounged up some wood and went to work. It was mostly done by the time I became aware of it. I watched as they tarred it to prevent leaks. Ok its ready to go. It was very heavy as it took 3 of them to carry it down to the marsh. I tagged along in anticipation, hoping they'd let me get in it too.

There was a little rundown pier there. The boat was gently placed in the water off the pier. So, it sat in the water on its flat bottom. I don't know if Harry wanted to be 1st in or he was elected. He seemed excited about it though. As he stepped one foot off the pier onto the "boat" it immediately flipped over flipping Harry into the water with it. First, I was afraid for him the he might be hurt, but turns out the water came just above his knees. Then I laughed & laughed at him! I don't think he chased or whipped me for laughing because I'm sure I'd remember. The stupid boat (if you call it that) is probably still there.

Life in Mentor-on-the-Lake was great. We boys would roam from our house all through the woods, marsh area, and all over the place. We even drank water right out of the little creek that ran through the woods.

We moved again to another rental house in 1958. Two things I remember about Harry during this time. One morning I was playing a Buddy Holly song "Every Day" on the record player over & over again. Harry was in the bathroom getting ready for school and told me to turn it off. I didn't. He came into the bedroom & gave me the worst whipping of my life. Needless to say, I never pushed him too far again.

Another time he and Randy got into a fight which was pretty big. I don't recall who got the best of it, I think Harry but can't be sure. I just remember trying to comfort the one laying on the glider on the front porch. Randy and Harry hung around each other the most as they were closer in age. When they had a fight it was usually a bad one.

I was away for a year and a half at a boy's correctional home, when I was able to come back home the family had moved to another home in Willoughby, Ohio. I started the 9th grade. Went to Jr. High School with Harry, didn't have any classes together but did see each other throughout the day. He was a real cool big brother. Harry was also very popular with the ladies. Unlike Randy whose relationships with ladies lasted a long time, Harry's had a life span of usually less than a month.

There was a time Harry talked me into playing the part of the big brother and double date at some girl's house. I don't remember her name or the reason for it. I was extremely uncomfortable and my "date" seemed to believe it. I was glad to go home. Harry told me I did well. He also showed me how to file down pennies to the size of a dime. They were good to use in pop machines & phone booths. He also showed me how to use phone booths for free. It only worked on the older phones.

Harry had a blue 55 Chevy that he would drive to school. He stopped going to school that year and went to get a job to help the family.

Harry and I had different friends and did different things. We did both go to a little hangout next to the Vine Theater in Willoughby. Played pinball & just hung out. It was said that if you wanted to find Harry that was the first place to look.

I again left home in 1963 to live at St. Anthony's Boy's Home. Once a month we had week-ends where we could leave after supper on Friday evenings & free until Sunday at 9 AM.

One time both Harry & Judy picked me up for my leave and brought me back to St. Anthony's in his 1958 Chevy Impala convertible.

Then I had to run away from St. Anthony's in the summer of 1964, it was Harry who helped me out. He gave me $10.00, and some advice. He said "If you don't want to get caught, don't do anything wrong." I actually followed that advice & vividly

151

remember it. He lived in an apartment with a buddy in downtown Cleveland at that time.

I went to Detroit and lived there off and on until I was drafted. I was excited when He & Judy came to Detroit to see me.

On one of my trips back to Ohio I stayed with Harry & Randy briefly in Berea.

I remember how he looked out for me when I was overseas.

Harry was a great story teller. Some of his comments would cut to the quick. I don't remember any long-winded advice, short and to the point that would make me think & usually helped me make the right choice.

It was always great to visit Harry. I think I was always proud to be his brother.

My brother Harry was a great 'big brother'. I was lucky to have this man in my life. Judy and his children lived with him longer than I. I envy them that.

When I see Joe, Rick & Paula I see that they are their father's children. Harry's success overcame a dysfunctional family life early in our lives. He was determined his children would not have that experience.

Judy, I credit you also for the persons your children are. Thank you for putting up with me on my late-night visits.

He was one of the coolest big brothers any person could hope for.

With much love,
Mike

Written by Milo, Foreign Exchange Student
December 2020

"I would like to say a few words about Harry.

An extraordinary and humble person, too hard to forget. Kindly, hard worker, a good father, husband and friend.

He was a nice person to talk with, always a smile on his face.

I am still remembering every moment shared with him and his lovely Family. He reminded me of both of my Grandparents, seemed to be educated by the same person. The value of the family and friendship was always his concern.

Too many moments shared with a beer in our hands in the living room warmed by the fire place, and his care for people, since the first day I arrived there, talking about different matters.

His love for the music, playing with his heart the piano.

His love for his family, the water, sky, our beautiful days spent at West Point Lake all together.

He always kept alive that little children we all have inside.

He was to me like a father to me, during the time I spent at your house, you all made me feel part of your family.

Harry left us a Legacy to all who knew him.

There are too many reasons why I will always love Harry and his entire family, for being so special, so kind, so human."

With all my love

Milo

Some Really Great Memories
Tony Boyd Priest
January 2021

Randy, Tony and Harry 1975

Harry and I first met in 1975 through Randy who had been taking flying lessons at Falcon Field, Peachtree City airport.

Randy had been training with me for some time and was getting close to his First Solo flight.

I had heard of Randy's family living in Peachtree City, got a name and number and called Harry to mention that his Brother might solo on the next training flight.

I suggested he come to the airport but remain out of sight and be ready with his camera. I didn't want to put any pressure on my Students in that regard.

Harry and Judy came over at the suggested time of course with cameras in hand. After I'd made a couple of trips around the pattern with Randy, sure enough, it was time for Randy's First Solo Flight.

I asked him to pull into the ramp, then opened my door, "Ok Randy, you can do it on your own. Just take it around the pattern again, pull back into the ramp when you get back. Call on the radio if you need anything."

He felt confident and was ready to go.

I got out of the still running aircraft, closed the door, patted on the side a couple of times and walked away.

Well, as Randy taxied out, Harry and Judy appeared. We met for the first time and they proceeded to film. We watched him depart and go out of sight for a few minutes then watched him return for his landing. He did it! A perfect landing!

It was a great First Solo Flight. A celebration was in order!

After that day we all became friends and later Harry and Judy joined my Aero Club.

It was initially through the Club, that we experienced some great times together.

One of our first flyway trips was to Ashville, North Carolina where the main attraction was the Vanderbilt Mansion. We had a great time there and began to realize more in common as our friendship developed.

Not many great pictures of that trip except for the group picture in front of the mansion.

Guess what. I'm not in it, just taking the picture.

Another great trip was to Hilton Head Island, South Carolina where we spent time at the beach and enjoyed some great meals at the Hotel.

Palmetto Dunes Hyatt, Hilton Head Island, South Carolina

We were circling to get a view of this brand-new Hyatt Hotel on the beach.

It was a beautiful day and our landing on the Island was great.

I can remember going through their amazing Buffet Line with Harry and Judy, and seeing Harry's face as he commented, "You know this is kind'a like 'Sport Eating'." We all laughed about that and enjoyed our time there immensely.

Another flight was to Albany, Georgia for a great Airshow. We all had a great time at the event.

On that particular flight they had to fly with one of our newer pilots for some reason. The flight down seemed fine. No Complaints.

However, that evening turned up some rather rough thunderstorms along with possibly the pilot may have gotten a little lost on the way home.

Well, they arrived back at Falcon Field about 30 minutes behind everyone else. We were all a little worried but as it turned out, not as bad as they were, along with the pilot's wife.

All three said they would never fly with him again!

Other than that, good memories of our time in the Aero Club, my first connection to the wonderful Glavosek Family.

FAMILIES GETTING TOGETHER

I believe it was their first Thanksgiving in Georgia when we invited them to celebrate at our home on Kings Ridge Road in Peachtree City.

We had Thanksgiving dinner outside on our Balcony which we all enjoyed tremendously. For an Ohio Family, that in itself seemed pretty amazing.

Later we built and had a great Bonfire in the backyard where I remember him asking, "You can really have a Bonfire in your backyard here?"

We later visited each other's homes on various occasions.

Our Kids played together and on one occasion, it was a Yahtzee game that he and Joe played against my Daughters, Suzanne and Andrea. Rick still has the score sheet!

Rick, yes, he's the one still hanging on to Willie Talk! I believe that's an amazing and great trait of a person...

Our sons eventually became involved in a Cub Scout Troup of which Judy was the Den Mother.

For their first Christmas in Georgia, we teamed up with the Wives and Kids to find their first Christmas Tree. We eventually found both our trees, beautiful full Cedars.

160

Rick and Joe probably remember following me through the rough washed-out terrain, their family in their pickup, me and my family in our stupid yellow Pinto 'jeep truck'.

Over the next few years, although in totally different occupations, we managed to have many adventures together. From boating (Harry gave me my first water ski lesson on Peachtree City Lake) "Boats with Motors Not Allowed" - to exploring together the open forests in Georgia.

From Derby Car Races to Christmas Caroling to Halloween, we did a lot together. Our little Quire of Scouts and myself on Guitar even entertained at a couple of Nursing Homes. Yes, we sang and enjoyed sing 'a longs' with the Old Folks.

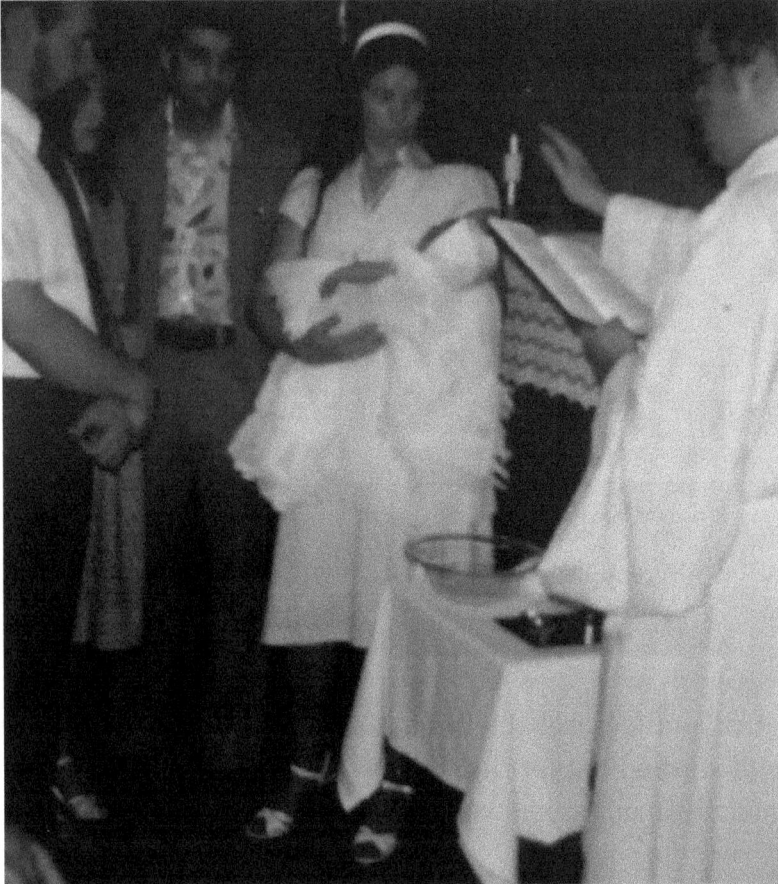

By this time, Harry and Judy had become our closest friends and as both families were attending Holy Trinity Church, we asked and they graciously accepted to stand up as God Parents for my Daughter Jennifer's Baptism.

A little later, at their home, Rick (or Ricky) let my young son Paul play with his Hot Wheels Collection. We all remember all his Hot Wheels lined up on the Fireplace Hearth, "Cars, Cars?"

The Fireplace brings to mind another amazing story.

162

THE BRICKS

Working as a Flight Instructor out of Falcon Field, I observed some of the ongoing grading and construction for a new Runway Extension.

One day, I noticed some black lines that didn't seem to fit into the normal smoothly graded red clay terrain. On subsequent flights I would check below me and finally counted 8 or 10 short symmetrical black lines.

After landing, I along with some of the folks working at the airport took a hike to see the lines up close.

Well to everyone's horror, the lines were 6 feet X 3 feet spaced 6 feet apart.

There was nothing there, until one of the guys found several square nails, then another found some old hinges. Whoops, Grave sites. Probably early 1800's as there was nothing left otherwise.

I alerted the airport folks to what had happened but obviously no one had any clue that was there.

Of course, always curious about such things, on subsequent flights, I scanned for any sign of ruins in the adjacent forest.

On one sunny day, lo and behold, I spotted on the top of a hill just above the gravesites what looked like some ruins of a home.

Who do I call...? my Adventure Mate... Harry Glavosek!

After discussing the situation and checking out maps, we decided to take a look.

At the time there were miles of forest between the paved road and where I'd viewed the ruins.

For a time, on additional flights I circled low in the area and eventually caught sight of what looked like an old wagon road which seemed to lead in the direction of the ruins.

I called Harry with the information and planned a preliminary scouting trip.

We met later, reviewed my aviation map notes and lines and finally identified a point to leave the pavement and civilization.

Then we headed home, that is to his house, and loaded up his truck with tools, shovels, and a chainsaw.

We were ready.

The next morning, I met up with Harry and the boys and headed out for our adventure.

Not long after leaving the pavement, we discovered the old ruts of a wagon road and proceeded with his pickup deeper into the forest.

By doing a little clearing along the way, including a couple of fairly large trees in the center of the wagon ruts, we finally made it to the top of the hill.

There it was!

A few pieces of a tin roof, pieces of an old stove, and a pile of old bricks obviously from a collapsed fire place. That was it.

After prodding around for a while, we decided to see if we could salvage any of the old bricks.

We shoveled away a lot of the debris and found the bricks continued deeper into the ground.

Seemed quite strange, however, the more we excavated, the more bricks we found and now they were in place as in a very large chimney.

At about the 4-foot level, we hit the bottom of the chimney and discovered there a large rock Fireplace Hearth!

We continued to excavate around the large 6-foot Hearth and found the very front of the structure. To our amazement the hearth was underneath that 4 feet of dirt!

I exclaimed, "Man this has got to be very, very old." Harry agreed.

What had started as a pile of Brick Rubble, turned into the Living Room of a home lost in antiquity.

Then, we both realized that the face of the fireplace had a huge oak tree probably 3 feet wide centered directly in front of the hearth.

After spending more time looking around the area, we decided there was nothing left except about a truck load of some like new bricks.

The boys had helped out all through the process, and now began helping us load the bricks aboard. Not sure how many but it was about all the pickup could handle.

The Beautiful Fireplace Harry built from the Bricks.

The Fireplace was only the Beginning!

Harry was very skilled in not only Body Shop work but was totally handy at creative construction.

It wasn't too long before he had built a beautiful Fireplace, yes totally constructed by using the 1800's Bricks.

Well, that began another incredible story. George!

Someone evidently came along from the old homestead with the Bricks to 233 Cedar Dr. Peachtree City, Ga.

George became his name, a little mischievous Boy Ghost!

Many incidents and sightings occurred in and around their home for several years.

That included visual sightings of the small boy in a Sailor Suit running around and once seen sitting on the mantel!

He slammed doors, opened and closed sliding doors, opened and closed cupboards, moved jewelry about and one time picked up a set of earrings several times and dropped them on an end table.

On one occasion, Joe and Rick were sitting at the bar as Mom was cooking breakfast.

As they sat waiting for their meal, the Salt and Pepper Shakers lifted up and were gently set back down onto the counter.

"Mom! Did you see that? She replied, "Yes I do!" She was quite shocked as they were.

More incidents occurred but I think the family got somewhat used to them.

Otherwise, they enjoyed the Fireplace and home for many years.

George was just an added colorful bonus to their busy lives, never hurting anyone!

Flight Over the Okefenokee Swamp

This little incident occurred on a flight down to Waycross, Georgia with Jim Sherrill as my student and Harry as a rear seat observer.

We were cruising along just talking and began discussing aerodynamics. I'd explained a few things to Jim, then told him I can show him how different pressures can be accomplished with the simple movement of the yoke.

I asked Jim, "Do you believe I can float that mike up out of its holder and wrap the cord around the yoke without touching it?"

"There's no way that can happen." he replied.

Harry was listening to all this aerodynamics talk and leaned up between the front seats to see if I could really do it.

I gently trimmed into a smooth descent, then with the increased airspeed began a smooth pull up.

Right at the best airspeed for the maneuver, I gently pushed over creating a solid negative G force.

Then the microphone lifted out of its holder and was approaching the yoke.

Suddenly, yelling began in the back.

Glancing over our shoulders... Harry was floating in the ceiling of the aircraft!

His back was against the top of the cabin.

I gently removed the negative pressure and he slowly lowered back into his seat!

It hadn't crossed my pea brain that in order for him to get between the front seats he would have to unbuckle his seat belt!!!

After everyone settled back to normal with seatbelts on. We began to laugh!

I sincerely apologized to Harry for not realizing he'd unbuckled!

We all had a terrific belly laugh out of the situation.

Later, as we were traveling along, I mentioned we were over the edge of the Okefenokee Swamp.

Guess what, they both wanted to take a little detour and do some aerial exploration.

A slight right turn and it wasn't long before we were deep into the swamp trying to spot alligators.

We got a little lower and sure enough began to see some wildlife.

Well during our tour, we spotted a Swamper Cabin along with a couple of old boats, yes, right in the middle of that dark water swamp.

Jim, "Let's get lower and see if we can see if anyone lives there."

"Well, Jim, Harry, keep an eye out if you see anybody with a Shotgun."

They agreed.

I got much lower and as we began to survey around the old cabin, Harry spotted two large alligators near the front porch.

A couple of moments later, it dawned on me that in this single engine aircraft, if we lost an engine, we'd be sitting in the middle of a dark water, alligator and snake filled swamp. There was nowhere to glide to! Prospects were not good at all for survival, even if we survived the crash.

I slowly added power, mentioned that to them, and slowly began a climb back toward civilization!

The more we talked about it the more a good lunch in Waycross, Georgia sounded.

All went well. Jim went to see his folks and Harry and I had lunch and rented a Car to be tourists for a while.

We had a great day kicking around the edge of the Okefenokee.

Our flight home was smooth and uneventful.

I certainly always enjoyed being around doing just about anything with 'Harry and Judy'. Great Friends that became Family!

MOVING AWAY

Although we'd grown to love Harry and Judy as our best friends, it was about June 1980 in pursuit of my Aviation Career that we moved away to California, then to Nevada, then on to Alaska.

We lived totally separate lives through the years as I moved around 'chasing airplanes'. However we remained good Friends through Christmas cards and letters.

We managed to visit from time to time but only briefly always remembering the good times.

I always thought of Harry as about my very Best Friend.

(On my return to Georgia in 2001, I was quite privileged to meet up with Paul, Harry's Dad again.

I spent the day with him in Warm Springs Georgia at the Little White House and then meticulously worked our way through the FDR Museum. It turned out that he knew a lot about "his Favorite President' and about the modified car he drove. It was a great day.)

I felt Honored, along with Judy, Paula and Granddaughters Meggan and Andrea to be one holding his Dad's hands as he Passed to join his son.

TONY PRIEST

Harry and Ruth

The Psalm on the following page was put together by Ruth and given to me (Judy) in Harry's Memory.

Blessings of the God-fearing man
Psalm 112

Praise ye the Lord. Blessed is the man who feareth the Lord, who delighteth greatly in His commandements.

His seed shall be mighty upon earth; the generation of the upright shall be blessed.

Wealth and riches shall be in his house; and his righteousness endureth forever.

Unto the upright there ariseth light in the darkness; he is gracious, and full of compassion, and righteous.

A good man showeth favor, and lendeth; he will guide his affairs with discretion.

Surely he shall not be moved forever; the righteous shall be in everlasting remembrance.

He shall not be afraid of evil tidings; his heart is fixed, trusting in the Lord.

His heart is secure, he will have no fear; in the end he will look in triumph on his foes.

He hath scattered abroad his gifts, he hath given to the poor; his righteousness endureth forever; his horn shall be exalted with honor.

IN LOVING MEMORY
of
J. HARRY GLAVOSEK

Husband, Father, Grandfather, Brother, Uncle, Friend......
Child of God

July 02, 1945
Aug. 30, 1991

This Cake was made by Jennifer Glavosek, Joes Wife, in celebration of Harry's Birthday we celebrated on the Cabin Cruiser!

REMEMBER THE GOOD TIMES!

Our son Richard, now 53 in 2021 still has Willie Talk!
A favorite Memory and Christmas Present. The old Accordion is
still in the Family!

Our Legacy Continues!

As of today's, writing, March 2021 Harry's and my Legacy continues to grow and change as most family's do. Due to births, deaths and even divorce, families are always changing and growing. Babies grow up, marry and have babies of their own. Our legacy is growing, to date there are twenty-eight of us.

Harry would be happy to know I have been happily married to Tony for going on twenty years. We have a good life together, making more memories.

Joe & Jen have a precious family of ten now. Their daughter Kira has two sons, Cameron and Tyler. Younger daughter and son-in-law, Kate & David have three children, Garrison, Jayna and Adalyn.

Rick is happily remarried to Laurie with a beautiful blended family of eight. Daughter & son-in-law, Andrea & Jacob & little baby Sadie, and son's Hunter, Alec and Colby.

Paula & Jeff have a precious family of eight, daughter and son-in-law, Meggan & Shane and little Savannah, daughter and son-in-law, Sarah & Preston and son Jeffery.

Each family is still continuing to grow!

"Thank You God for our beautiful precious Family!"

HEY KIDS… NO EXCUSES. "DON'T SAY I CAN'T!"

JUST GET OUT AND DO IT! YOU <u>CAN</u> DO IT!

Diary SATERDAY

I have been hear about 3½ months. It is January 9, 1960. I came in Sept. 25, 1959. Right now I have head aks. It is about 6:30 P.M. Every time, when I am home, and I feal like getting in trouble I will look at this card and read it. I miss my fainly and friends and fainly. The cottage whent went off the hill roller shating last moneday. It was the first time I was off the hill sience I been hear. Right now I am lost and it seems like I an not ever going home. I will never be a second time.

BIT DUM

I WISH I WAS HOME

Harry Glavorek

B. I. S.

I WANA TO GO HOME

1½ more more months to go I hope.

THIS IS A REMINDER NOT TO GET IN TROUBLE

B.I.S. - Boy's Industrial School, Lancaster, Ohio

www.ingramcontent.com/pod-product-compliance
Lightning Source LLC
Chambersburg PA
CBHW060923040426
42445CB00011B/769